CH6MPIONS

★★★ OF EUROPE ★★★

CH6MPIONS

★★★ OF EUROPE ★★★

Reach Sport

CH6MPIONS OF EUROPE

Hardback edition first published in Great Britain in 2019
www.reachsport.com
@reach_sport
Reach Sport is a part of Reach PLC Ltd, 5 St Paul's Square, Liverpool, L3 9SJ
One Canada Square, Canary Wharf, London, E15 5AP

Hardback ISBN: 9781911613473

Photographic acknowledgements:
Liverpool FC Getty Images, PA, Mirrorpix, Tony Woolliscroft

Editor: David Cottrell
Design: Colin Sumpter
Production Editor: Michael McGuinness
Sub Editor: Roy Gilfoyle
Writers: David Cottrell, William Hughes, Chris McLoughlin, Michael McGuinness

Printed and bound by Bell & Bain Ltd

Istanbul
The Final 2005
The Final 2005

THIS LIVERPOOL NEVER STOPS. THIS LIVERPOOL NEVER QUITS. THIS LIVERPOOL GIVES EVERYTHING AT ALL TIMES. WHATEVER HAPPENS THIS LIVERPOOL LEAVES IT ALL ON THE PITCH AND NOTHING LEFT FOR REGRETS. WE DON'T DO 'IF ONLY'"

FINAL
MADRID 2019

CONTENTS

THE ONE THAT GOT AWAY, AND
THE ONE THAT FELT LIKE FATE…

PROLOGUE

THE WALK OF CHAMP
Achievement runs through our veins... It's part of our DNA. In our inaugural season of 1892-93 Liverpool Football Club won the Lancashire League. Just eight years later,
18
European Cup/
UEFA Champions
League
5
UEFA
Cup
3
League
Cup
Ma
L.F.C.

It had just gone five o'clock on Sunday 12 May 2019 and the Liverpool FC first-team squad and their families, along with the coaching staff, were on the pitch at Anfield in the late-afternoon sunshine, saluting the full house that had stayed behind after the 2-0 win over Wolverhampton Wanderers on the final day of the Premier League season.

Despite accumulating 97 points, a total bettered by only three teams in top-flight history (adjusted to three-points-for-a-win), the Premier League title had eluded Jürgen Klopp's side.

It was an agonisingly close way to come second after such a sensational domestic season, but there were no long faces among the players or fans – only smiles and singing and excitement for what lay ahead.

The Reds had raised the bar in the 2018/19 Premier League. It was the best points-per-game ratio (at 2.55) in the club's top-flight history. Liverpool had gone 20 games without defeat from the beginning of the campaign and were unbeaten at home for a second successive league season.

They'd been the last team in the top four divisions of English football to lose a league fixture in 2018/19, and they'd lost just once.

Mo Salah became the quickest player to 50 league goals in LFC history, doing so in 69 fixtures. He also shared the

Premier League Golden Boot with Sadio Mane, the duo scoring 22 goals apiece.

Goalkeeper Alisson won the Premier League Golden Glove for keeping most clean-sheets, with 21, in his debut campaign with the Reds.

Centre-half Virgil van Dijk was named the PFA Players' player of the year, a year after Salah had claimed the same accolade. The big Dutchman was joined by Trent Alexander-Arnold, Andy Robertson and Sadio Mane in the PFA team of the year.

It felt good among the fans too. Anfield recorded a club-record average home league attendance of 53,174 (beating the 53,113 set two seasons earlier) and enjoyed a club-record highest aggregate attendance in a single season of 1,010,316 (beating the previous best of 1,010,170 from back in 1972/73).

Unity was most definitely strength, and nowhere was this more evident than when Liverpool were playing in Europe. Four-and-a-bit days before the Wolves win, Anfield had witnessed another epoch-defining comeback as Liverpool beat Barcelona 4-0 in the second leg of their Champions League semi-final.

In doing so they became only the third team in history to overturn a three-goal first-leg deficit at this stage of

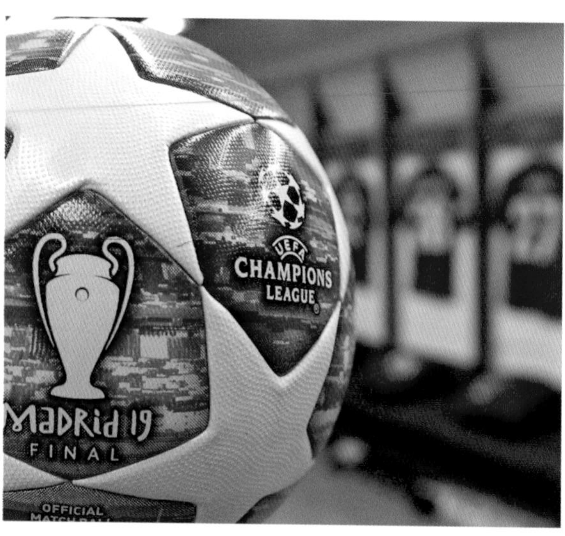

European football's elite competition and the show of solidarity at the end of the night summed up everything about LFC, its players, coaching team and supporters.

In his subsequent matchday programme notes (for Wolves) Jürgen Klopp wrote: "I was asked in the post-match press-conference if Liverpool could have won the tie if we played in a stadium without any supporters. My answer was 'no chance' but it made me reflect on how blessed those of us who work here are...

"This is Liverpool now: a powerful collective who looks to live in the moment and embrace the joy of it.

"Thank you Anfield – you are special."

It was the season when Jürgen fired final-whistle fist-pumps at a raucous Kop as his red juggernaut gathered pace; when we marked the 30th anniversary of Hillsborough, celebrated the 100th anniversary of Bob Paisley's birth and said goodbye to Tommy Smith; when Kenny Dalglish was knighted at Buckingham Palace and Reds legends raised funds for the LFC Foundation then the Sean Cox Rehabilitation Trust.

But would it end on a high? After going so close in the league at home, and after the Champions League heartache of Kiev the previous year, would there be a silver lining to the season finale?

ANFIELD, SEPTEMBER 2018, WHERE IT ALL BEGAN...

L.F.C.
1

UEFA
CHAMPIONS
LEAGUE
adidas

Inside the home dressing-room ahead of the PSG game with a new group-stage ball to play with

The Paris squad at Anfield the night before

Stand
PS4 Pro
NISSAN
mastercard
GAZPROM
Hotels.com

Brazilian ace Neymar with club and country colleagues Marquinhos and Thiago Silva

PARIS

L.F.C.
Fly

1

Allez les Rouges

Liverpool v Paris Saint-Germain

Sitting in the depths of the NSC Olimpiyskiy Stadium in Kiev, Jürgen Klopp cut a disconsolate figure. Liverpool had just lost in their first Champions League final for over a decade as Real Madrid lifted the trophy for the third time in a row following a 3-1 victory.

Klopp's side actually played well on that balmy Ukrainian evening but had been undone by two goals they shouldn't have conceded and one they could do very little, truth be told, to prevent.

As he addressed the world's media afterwards, the Liverpool manager had already made a conscious decision not to let the defeat linger.

He later explained: "I actually decided that night that it would not really...keep me. You saw the game. It happened like it happened. What can you do? Yes, disappointment, being sad, all that stuff. But when we arrived in England again, I was already over it."

Many pundits doubted Klopp's side would be competing in European football's showpiece occasion again any time soon and questions were inevitably raised about how the players would react to such a disappointment.

Two months later, left-back Andy Robertson admitted that doing so would stretch the team's mental toughness to its limits.

Sitting in the reception area at Melwood, the club's West Derby training headquarters, with a shiny European Cup encased in a presentation cabinet behind him, the Scotland international admitted: "I'm probably still not over it, to be honest. I don't think the lads will get over it.

"It'll be something where you'll always have those 'what ifs' in your head and it could have been a very different outcome. But I think it will get easier to move on from, the more games we play.

"At the very start of the tournament probably nobody thought that Liverpool would be there in the final, but we believed in ourselves. If you had said at the start of last season that we'd get to the Champions League final, I think a lot of our fans would have bitten your hand off given the quality of the teams that have been there and done it in that competition over the last couple of years when we'd struggled to qualify.

"But we have shown that we can compete against the best and we can take a lot of confidence from that and hopefully we can take that into this new season."

As a club, Liverpool were determined to move on from the pain of Kiev quickly. Just hours after the defeat by Real Madrid the Reds announced that the Brazilian midfielder Fabinho would be their first summer signing.

And while the clickbait websites and newspaper gossip columns habitually link the Reds with numerous new recruits, this was a move that had genuinely gone under the radar.

Klopp, looking to add strength in depth to his squad and needing a midfield replacement for Juventus-bound Emre Can, wasted no time in bringing in the 24-year-old Monaco man for a reported fee of £39 million.

"He has ability and mentality to play at the highest level in a number of positions," said the boss. "He can play 'six', 'eight' and 'two'. This is cool."

Fabinho himself was delighted at moving to the Champions League runners-up:

"This is something that I always wanted – this is a giant

THIS IS
LIVER POOL
FOOTBALL CLUB
ANFIELD

MEANS MORE
WE ARE

of a team. I am really excited. A football club of this size coming after my services, I didn't have to think that much about coming over.

"I will try to create my own history at this football club. Hopefully, on a personal level, I'm able to win titles with this club."

Fabinho's formal transfer went through on 1 July 2018, enabling him to join fellow midfield addition Naby Keita when the team reconvened for pre-season training.

By the middle of the month Liverpool had made two further moves into the transfer market.

The first saw them add Stoke City's Swiss international attacker Xherdan Shaqiri for a bargain price of £13.75 million following the Potters' relegation to the Championship.

But it was their final piece of business which aroused the most interest. After experiencing such a difficult time of it in the Champions League final, goalkeeper Loris Karius' future became clearer when the Reds made AS Roma number one Alisson Becker the most expensive keeper in Britain, splashing out a reported £66.8 million on the Brazilian. It would prove to be a very significant signing.

"I'm really happy, it's a dream-come-true to wear such a prestigious shirt for a club of this size that is used to always winning," Alisson told the club's website after completing the deal.

"In terms of my life and my career, it's a huge step for me being part of this club and this family. You can be certain I will be giving it my all.

"Hopefully I can play a part in the history being created here, win titles and be a part of the project that has been developed here in the past few years so we can see Liverpool rise once again."

Klopp paid tribute to the club's owners for backing him to complete the somewhat serendipitous deal once it became clear Alisson might be available.

"At one point in the last few weeks it came up, the opportunity to sign one of the world's best goalkeepers. The owners were quite excited, so we did it. He [Alisson] has nothing to do with the price, we have nothing to do with the price. It's the market, that's how it is and we will not think a lot about it.

"He needs to adapt to the English Premier League. The league is different, the refs are different, the goalkeeper's life is different in the Premier League.

"We got him here because of his existing strengths, which is in all goalkeeper departments the highest level."

The boss watching the Paris players warming up ahead of kick-off

By virtue of finishing fourth in the Premier League, the Reds had qualified for Europe's premier club tournament again. By the time the draw was made on 30 August, they had made a perfect start to their Premier League campaign with three wins out of three, seeing off West Ham United, Crystal Palace and Brighton & Hove Albion.

Midfielder Gini Wijnaldum explained: "We have to keep concentrated and deal with every situation that will come. We feel good and we're going to try to feel as good for a long time."

Liverpool were handed a tricky-looking Champions League assignment, being placed in Group C along with French champions Paris Saint-Germain, Italian heavyweights Napoli and Serbian title-holders Red Star Belgrade.

The clash with the Parisians was the most mouthwatering and would also be the tie to kick-off both teams' interest in the tournament, with the game being scheduled for Anfield on 18 September.

It was over 20 years since the sides had last met in a competitive match with Liverpool, then managed by Roy Evans, suffering the disappointment of a semi-final exit in what was then the European Cup Winners' Cup. A 2-0 win at Anfield wasn't enough to overturn a 3-0 reverse in the Parc des Princes a fortnight earlier.

This time around, the interest centred on the clubs' respective front-threes. Liverpool's attacking trident of Mo Salah, Sadio Mane and Roberto Firmino had done so much to catapult them to the latter stages of the 2017/18 competition. Lining-up against them were the much-vaunted trio of Brazilian superstar Neymar, the prolific Uruguayan Edinson Cavani and the electric-heeled French teenager Kylian Mbappe.

Legendary forward Thierry Henry had been particularly taken by his countryman, saying in one interview: "I don't like comparing players – Mbappe has to become Mbappe and that is all. But my word, he is good. *Ooh la la!* I really like watching him play."

By the time the Champions League music was ringing around Anfield again, Liverpool had stretched their 100 per cent league record to five out of five. PSG, who like the Reds were managed by an ex-Borussia Dortmund coach in Thomas Tuchel, were setting the pace in Ligue 1 – also with a perfect record after five fixtures.

Visiting captain Thiago Silva was expecting a fiercely-contested Champions League group. "It's the Champions League and if we want to go far we have to beat very good teams," said the Brazilian.

Champions League anthem time

Three photos that say: we mean business

"I know my team is ready for this challenge and that's the most important thing. Liverpool and Red Star Belgrade are clubs that have made their mark in football, with great atmospheres and the atmosphere is also red-hot in Naples. We'll have to be very focused to win there.

"We must have a lot of respect for our three opponents but we mustn't forget our qualities. Our aim is to finish top of the group, but it won't be easy against these quality opponents."

Klopp, meanwhile, was every bit as excited as the supporters at the prospect of seeing his side pit their wits against the French aristocrats.

"PSG are one of the favourites for the competition that's for sure," he said in his pre-match press-briefing. "This team is built for winning the Champions League. It will be an interesting game for sure. With the players they have and the manager they have, they all brought it together to go as far as possible in the Champions League and we are aware of that.

"Winning the first game is always an advantage, but we haven't won it yet – we have to play it and it will be really difficult."

Sometimes high-profile games do not live up to the hype. This was not one of those occasions. Supporters sat captivated as both sides went at breakneck speed for the 90-plus minutes. It was breathless entertainment with thrills and spills aplenty and, like any good story, a late twist.

Firmino was not deemed fit to start after sustaining an eye injury in the Premier League win over Tottenham at Wembley the previous weekend, but that didn't prevent him from becoming the game's central figure as his injury-time goal at the Anfield Road end helped Liverpool to triumph by the odd goal in five.

For Tuchel there was an unmistakable sense of *deja-vu*. The German coach had been in charge of Dortmund when they lost 4-3 to the Reds at Anfield in an epic 2016 Europa League quarter-final second leg, courtesy of a last minute Dejan Lovren winner. Now his PSG side had suffered the same fate.

In a move that raised smiles among the jubilant Liverpudlians inside Anfield, Firmino celebrated his last-gasp decider by placing a hand over the eye he had injured against Spurs.

Fly
RESPECT
14
PARIS

Mo Salah motors with Juan Bernat in pursuit

"The score wasn't logical," said Tuchel afterwards.

"It was a crazy game but this is Anfield, this is what they do." He was right on all three counts as Liverpool would have won by more had the score been logical, but on this crazy Champions League night – with PSG's fanatical support adding to the colour of the evening's outstanding atmosphere – it played out as an intense five-goal thriller.

Daniel Sturridge, starting in place of Firmino, headed in Robertson's brilliant cross to get things underway on the half-hour mark before Wijnaldum was tripped in the penalty area and James Milner – who had set the tone for the night with a crunching early tackle on Neymar – stroked home the penalty.

The Guardian reported that PSG were struggling to stem the red tide at this point in proceedings. "The team in red played as if affronted by the suggestion that the opposition had the better selection of attacking riches.

"Liverpool did not reach the final last season with conservatism and, once again, they could be seen trying to rush the opposition players off their feet, swarming forward and, in the first half, rekindling the thought it is amazing how many times European opponents concede a goal in front of the Kop, become unnerved and quickly let in another one."

PSG were back in business before half-time, though, when right-back Thomas Meunier fired home after the assistant-referee failed to spot Cavani straying offside in the build up [VAR was introduced later in the competition].

Trent holds off a challenge from Edinson Cavani

Standard
Chartered

Daniel Sturridge's superbly-taken header opens the scoring for the hosts

Mo Salah then had a goal somewhat harshly disallowed for a foul by Sturridge on goalkeeper Alphonse Areola and that looked like being costly when Neymar created an 83rd-minute leveller for Mbappe, who surged into the box and lifted the ball past Alisson.

But Firmino had Anfield rocking when defenders Joe Gomez and Virgil van Dijk combined to find him and he darted past centre-back Marquinhos before sending a low, angled drive into the bottom corner in the 91st minute to give the Reds a well-deserved win on yet another exhilarating European night at Anfield.

It also meant Liverpool had won their opening six

games of the season for the first time since 1961 in the old Second Division. How Tuchel must have wished that LFC were still down there!

Klopp felt the result showed how much the Reds had progressed since he was appointed manager in October 2015.

"When you hear Liverpool are playing PSG, you don't think Liverpool don't stand a chance any more," he said. "That wasn't the case two or three years ago. What the boys made of our match-plan was outstanding. Against PSG you can't play with 95 per cent. If you play to your full capacity, you can win the game."

Ex-Reds defender Stephen Warnock saluted the team for their willingness to go to the final whistle. He told Radio Five Live: "When PSG equalised in the 83rd minute I was thinking 'well, this is a draw now' but Liverpool still pushed forward for a winner.

"You could argue it was a dangerous way to play,

especially against a team of that quality, but Klopp wanted the three points and he got them thanks to Firmino's stoppage-time strike."

Mirror journalist Andy Dunn praised unsung heroes such as Milner, who had topped the Champions League goalscoring assists standings in 2017/18, and pinpointed the way the vice-captain had helped set the tempo for the victory.

"It was the sort of night when the intensity of James Milner and his team-mates was ultimately too much for Parisian style," he wrote.

"Yes, the dramatic final act was provided by Roberto Firmino, who rendered Kylian Mbappe's equaliser meaningless with his superb added-time winner. But another spine-tingling Anfield night belonged as much to the likes of Milner as it did to Firmino."

Meanwhile, a delighted Robertson explained that there was nothing quite like a last-minute winner.

"It was unbelievable and a great night at Anfield again," he said soon after the final whistle. Ever since the disappointment of last May we've been waiting for these Champions League nights to return.

The man of the moment celebrates in Studge style with team-mates and fans

L.F.C.
RESPECT
RESPECT
5
15

Fly
Emirates

"IT WAS THE SORT OF NIGHT WHEN THE INTENSITY OF JAMES MILNER AND HIS LIVERPOOL TEAM-MATES WAS ULTIMATELY TOO MUCH FOR PARISIAN STYLE"

James Milner makes no mistake
from the spot and it's two-nil

"Since we reported back for pre-season, we have been hungry for all the games to come around. Fortunately we didn't disappoint and it was good to get the three points and off to a good start in the group."

Elsewhere on Matchday One, Tottenham Hotspur and Manchester City both made losing starts. Spurs went down 2-1 to Inter Milan in the San Siro after conceding twice in the final five minutes, while City fell to a shock 2-1 defeat against Lyon at the Etihad Stadium with first-half goals from Maxwel Cornet and Nabil Fekir proving enough for the French side to claim victory.

Manchester rivals United were 3-0 winners against Young Boys in Bern with Paul Pogba scoring twice for Jose Mourinho's side.

Over in Spain, holders Real Madrid made a fine start in their quest for a fourth successive triumph, beating AS Roma 3-0 in the Santiago Bernabeu, while Barcelona thrashed PSV Eindhoven 4-0 at the Nou Camp with the Champions League's top scorer, Lionel Messi, settling into his usual groove with a hat-trick.

Next on the Reds' continental calendar were a couple of October engagements, first in Naples and then back in L4 against Red Star. But as Kopites left Anfield with a spring in their step there was an almost tangible sense that this result might prove important.

Liverpool were on the march again.

Allez les Rouges.

LIVERPOOL 3
PARIS SAINT-GERMAIN 2

Anfield - Group C Matchday One

Tuesday 18 September 2018 - Kick-off 8pm

Goals: Sturridge (30), Milner (36 pen), Meunier (40), Mbappe (83), Firmino (90)

LIVERPOOL (4-3-3):
Alisson, Alexander-Arnold, Gomez, Van Dijk, Robertson, Henderson (C), Wijnaldum, Milner, Sturridge (Firmino 72), Mane (Fabinho 90), Salah (Shaqiri 85). Subs not used: Mignolet, Keita, Moreno, Matip. Booked: Van Dijk.

PSG (4-3-3):
Areola, Meunier, Kimpembe, Thiago Silva (C), Bernat, Marquinhos, Rabiot, Di Maria (Draxler 80), Cavani (Choupo-Moting 80), Mbappe, Neymar. Subs not used: Cibois, Kehrer, L Diarra, Nkunku, Nsoki. Booked: Meunier.

Attendance: 52,478. Referee: Cuneyt Cakir.

Standard Chartered
LFC

Standard Chartered
9
14
7
12
Fly Emirates

The visitors on the offensive

Kylian Mbappe beats goalie Alisson to make it two-two on the night – can the Reds respond?

Bobby's canvas and a stroke of genius wins it

Fly
Emirates
66

Firmino: the finish and the fun

L.F.C.
Standard
RESPECT

L.F.C.
Standard Chartered
14
L.F.C.
L.F.C.

L.F.C.
Standard
RESPECT
26

Final whistle: when the Reds win, we all win

NAPLES, BELGRADE, PARIS… NOW GET OUT OF THAT

L.F.C.
2

The Reds starting XI in Naples

SANGUE
AZZURRO
ASSOCIAZIONE ITALIANA
NAPOLI CLUB
Standard Chartered

Standard Chartered
LFC

It just got tougher

Napoli v Liverpool, Liverpool v Red Star, Red Star v Liverpool & PSG v Liverpool

The home win over PSG provided Liverpool with the perfect platform to build upon in Group C, especially with Napoli and Red Star sharing the spoils with a goalless draw in Belgrade.

Next for Jürgen Klopp and his side was a trip to Naples. Liverpool's unbeaten start had come to an end a week earlier when Chelsea won a Capital One Cup third-round tie at Anfield 2-1 thanks to a late piece of genius by substitute Eden Hazard.

Hazard also scored when the teams met again at Stamford Bridge three days later in a Premier League clash, but Daniel Sturridge's brilliant late equaliser kept the Reds' unbeaten league start intact and Klopp would later be named as the Premier League's manager of the month for September.

Liverpool knew that the trip to the intimidating Stadio San Paolo in southern Italy would be a tough one but also that victory would put them in a strong position in the standings going into their back-to-back clashes with Red Star on matchdays three and four.

In his pre-match press conference in Campania, Klopp noted a switch in the Italians' tactics since the great Carlo Ancelotti had replaced Maurizio Sarri as manager the previous summer.

"They have changed their style and lost Jorginho, but they're very quick upfront, they have good footballers, a good counter-press, a good counter... It will be interesting."

Yet for once, in an otherwise thrilling 2018/19 season, it wasn't. There were very few poor performances by Liverpool throughout the campaign but this would be one of them.

Liverpool Echo correspondent James Pearce described the team as "abject from start to finish. It was hard to believe this was a team which had beaten Paris Saint-Germain a fortnight earlier and is level at the top of the Premier League with Manchester City.

"After such a promising start to the campaign, standards dipped alarmingly."

At least the travelling fans were under cover

No way through for Sadio and Bobby

On a wet and blustery night, it still looked like a resolute defensive display had done enough to earn a point for Klopp's side only for Napoli forward Lorenzo Insigne to supply a 90th-minute sting in the tail that had the Stadio San Paolo erupting like Mount Vesuvius just six miles away.

Ancelotti's side worked the ball down the left for Spaniard Jose Callejon to get in behind the Reds defence and he played in a low cross for local lad and Italian international Insigne to slide in at the far post. It was a bitter pill to swallow, although Liverpool could have no complaints.

"The defeat is deserved, so we don't have to make a big story of it," was Klopp's honest assessment and it was hard to disagree. Losing Naby Keita to a back injury in the opening 20 minutes didn't help, but the Reds never got going and their failure to produce a shot on target for the first time in a Champions League game since a 1-0 defeat at Benfica in 2006 said it all.

Aside from Keita's setback, little of note happened before the interval. Insigne fired one low shot wide. But the home side, who had scored against every English team they'd faced at Stadio San Paolo bar Liverpool in 2010, assumed control after the break. Alisson was called into action to make a save from Arkadiusz Milik – hold that thought – and the outstanding Joe Gomez cleared Callejon's effort off the line.

At the other end a Mo Salah curler that drifted wide of the post was as close as Liverpool came.

Mo would have no joy against the impressive Kalidou Koulibaly…on this occasion

Lete
26

NISSAN
EQUAL GAME
RESPECT
CHAMPIONS LEAGUE

Standard Chartered
LFC

HB
007

Standard Chartered
Lete

Substitute Dries Mertens should have broken the deadlock in the 82nd minute when he met Mario Rui's wicked low cross full-on but he only managed to shin the ball against the crossbar before Virgil van Dijk shrewdly eased Insigne away from the rebound.

That appeared to be enough to secure a point but whereas Roberto Firmino had struck a late winner against PSG on the Group C opening night, this time it was the Reds on the end of a last-ditch goal that turned a frustrating night into a bad one.

Former Reds winger Steve McManaman, working as a pundit for BT Sport, explained: "I said before the game that if Liverpool got a draw you'd be happy with it, but they lost with a couple of minutes to go. It was very much safety-first, they just got caught near the end.

"If it had finished 0-0 and that goal hadn't happened then the manager would've been disappointed with the performance but thrilled with the result. That's the dangerous game you play."

Reds central defender Van Dijk admitted: "To be honest this was probably the first defeat we've had this season where we thought we did deserve to lose.

"But when you are nil-nil in the last couple of minutes you want to grind out the result and take a point back with you.

"So we were disappointed but we weren't good enough on the night. Everyone knew it. We spoke about it afterwards and we want to bounce back as quickly and as well as possible."

Other highlights on Matchday Two saw Barcelona beat Spurs at Wembley, CSKA shock Real Madrid in Moscow and Neymar hit a hat-trick as PSG thrashed Red Star 6-1 to move level on points with the Reds and Napoli at the top of Group C.

Napoli celebrate with their fans, Jürgen grins and bears it

NAPOLI 1
LIVERPOOL 0

Stadio San Paolo - Group C Matchday Two
Wednesday 3 October 2018 - Kick-off 8pm
Goal: Insigne (90)

NAPOLI (4-3-3):
Ospina, Maksimovic, Albiol, Koulibaly, Mario Rui, Allan, Hamsik (C) (Zielinski 81), Ruiz (Verdi 68), Callejon, Milik (Mertens 68), Insigne. Subs not used: Karnezis, Hysaj, Rog, Diawara. Booked: Koulibaly.

LIVERPOOL (4-3-3):
Alisson, Alexander-Arnold, Gomez, Van Dijk, Robertson, Wijnaldum, Milner (C) (Fabinho 76), Keita (Henderson 19), Firmino, Mane (Sturridge 89), Salah. Subs not used: Mignolet, Lovren, Moreno, Shaqiri. Booked: Milner.

Attendance: 37,057. Referee: Viktor Kassai.

Liverpool's chance to atone for their setback in Naples came three weeks later when Red Star Belgrade were the visitors to Anfield.

Klopp's men went into the clash knowing that all the fans in the stadium would be behind them – literally. Red Star supporters were banned by UEFA from visiting Anfield for the tie following previous crowd trouble, with the Liverpool manager revealing before the game that such a situation would be a new one for him.

"I have never experienced a stadium full of only one crowd," he said. "The support here in England is different, especially at Anfield it's different. We don't sing against another crowd. It's a little bit like that, but it's more that you follow the game and support your team.

"If we have a bigger number, cool. It's all about being really together tomorrow. We have to make sure that this one advantage that we can have in our home games – our crowd – is there 100 per cent. I'm pretty sure they are ready. This is only a little reminder!"

The away-fan ban and a Main Stand power-cut made it a strange Anfield Champions League night off the pitch but it was business as usual on it. Liverpool won 4-0 and their electric front-three supplied the goals.

Supporters of Red Star Belgrade – or Crvena Zvezda, to give them their non-Anglicised name – watching on television saw their side comprehensively beaten with the only gripe being that Klopp's Reds

Kop that - but no visiting fans to witness it

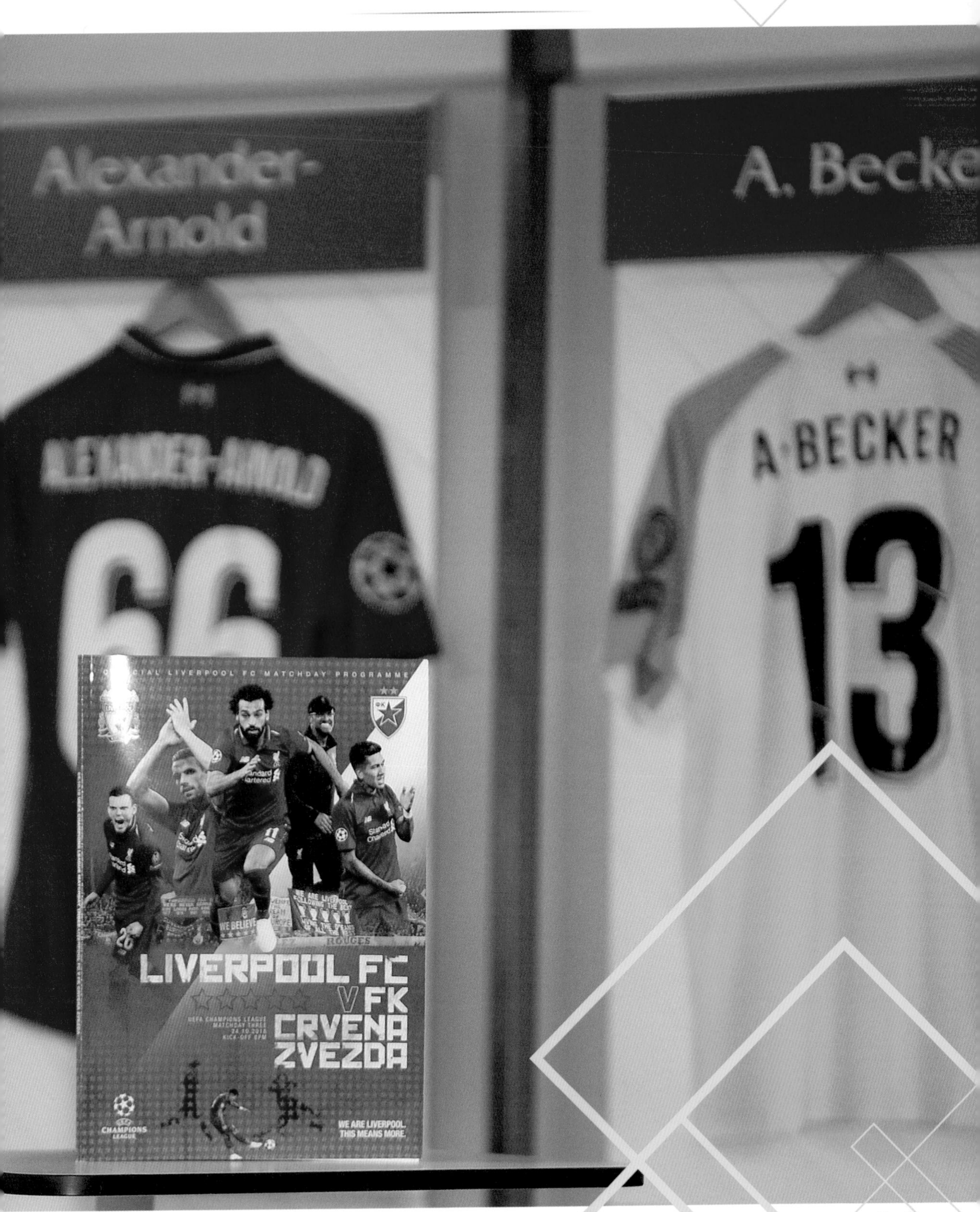
Alexander-
Arnold
A. Becke
ALEXANDER-ARNOLD
66
A.BECKER
13
OFFICIAL LIVERPOOL FC MATCHDAY PROGRAMME
LIVERPOOL FC
V FK
CRVENA
ZVEZDA
CHAMPIONS LEAGUE
WE ARE LIVERPOOL.
THIS MEANS MORE.

EST·1892
LIVERPOOL
FOOTBALL CLUB
YOU'LL NEVER WALK ALONE

PS4 Pro
NISSAN

macron
MANÉ
BABIĆ
15

should have scored more than four.

Xherdan Shaqiri, playing in a deeper midfield role, was at his creative best and it was the Swiss international who opened up Red Star for both first-half goals, supplying a brilliant defence-splitting pass for Andy Robertson to pull back to Firmino to convert and then slipping Salah in for a thumping right-footed finish.

That was the Egyptian King's 49th goal for LFC in his 65th appearance and it only took six minutes of the second half for the 50th to arrive.

Salah fired home a penalty down the centre of the goal after Sadio Mane had been face-palmed by Red Star skipper Filip Stojkovic in the box.

Mane himself had the opportunity to make it 4-0 from the spot following a daft handball by forward El Fardou Ben Nabouhane but goalkeeper Milan Borjan brilliantly pushed the ball against the crossbar.

However the Canadian international couldn't keep Mane out in the 80th minute of the match after he had been teed up by fellow striker Daniel Sturridge. Four-nil, game over.

Twenty on the clock as Bobby fires the hosts into the lead

"I'M VERY HAPPY ABOUT SCORING 50 GOALS FOR LIVERPOOL. THE MOST IMPORTANT THING THOUGH IS THE TEAM – I HOPE WE CAN WIN THE CHAMPIONS LEAGUE"

66
11
5

Pro
66

LFC
Standard
Chartered

With Fabinho, on his first European start, and Gini Wijnaldum bossing the midfield and captain-for-the-night Van Dijk in commanding form alongside Gomez at the back, the visitors never looked like scoring and Liverpool ended the night top of Group C after PSG and Napoli shared a 2-2 draw in Paris.

Writing in the *Liverpool Echo*, ex-Reds midfielder Jan Molby said: "Red Star are the weakest team in the group but you still have to beat them and Liverpool did that in style. You've got to say that the scoreline flattered Red Star. Liverpool should have had a few more goals but overall it was a very pleasing night."

Salah told UEFA: "I'm very happy about scoring 50 goals for Liverpool. The most important thing though is the team. I'm very happy that I was able to help them win the match. I hope we can win [the Champions League]. There's a long way to go, but I hope we can continue to play well and do what we did last season."

Mane makes it four with his first of the 2018/19 tournament

LIVERPOOL 4
RED STAR BELGRADE 0

Anfield Group C - Matchday Three
Wednesday 24 October 2018 - Kick-off 8pm
Goals: Firmino (20), Salah (45, 51 pen), Mane (80)

LIVERPOOL (4-3-3):
Alisson, Alexander-Arnold, Gomez, Van Dijk (C), Robertson (Moreno 82), Fabinho, Wijnaldum, Shaqiri (Lallana 68), Firmino, Salah (Sturridge 73), Mane. Subs not used: Mignolet, Lovren, Milner, Origi.

RED STAR (4-2-3-1):
Borjan, Stojkovic (C), Babic, Degenek, Gogeljic, Krsticic, Jovicic (Causic 75), Srnic, Ebecilio (Jovancic 65), Ben (Simic 80), Boakye. Subs not used: Popovic, Pavkov, Stoiljkovic, Savic. Booked: Stojkovic, Krsticic, Jovicic, Jovancic, Gobeljic.

Attendance: 53,024. Referee: Daniel Siebert.

Standard Chartered

Before the Reds' next Champions League night on home soil, they faced the return trips to Belgrade and Paris. Those Champions League ambitions of Salah and his team-mates would be shaken as the away-day issue that first reared its head in Naples continued to afflict them.

First came a 2-0 defeat in Belgrade. The fixture was Liverpool's 200th game in the European Cup/Champions League but their first in Serbia since the country gained independence from the former Republic of Yugoslavia.

On their biggest Champions League night in Belgrade since they were European Champions in 1991, Red Star's vociferous supporters welcomed Liverpool to the atmospheric Stadion Rajko Mitic by creating a mural that translated as 'Let There Be A Constant Battle'.

It was a battle their team won as the Reds slipped to a third consecutive away defeat in this competition for the first time since 1979, with the hostile atmosphere – which included the choreographed chanting of a rude phrase best described as telling Liverpool where to go – inspiring Crvena Zvezda to victory and showing why their home is nicknamed 'Marakana' after the famous stadium in Brazil.

Without Shaqiri, who remained on Merseyside to avoid the possibility of any politically-motivated distractions, and Dejan Lovren, who was unwell, Klopp brought Adam Lallana and Joel Matip into his team with Sturridge selected ahead of Firmino upfront.

RESPECT
66

Had Sturridge not blazed a gilt-edged opportunity over the bar early in the first half things may well have been different. But his uncharacteristic profligacy set the tone for a night of missed chances – later described by Klopp as "scruffy situations" – at one end while Milan Pavkov punished Liverpool at the other.

The Serbian striker netted twice in the space of eight minutes, his first a header from a corner and the second a powerful effort that flew past Alisson from 30 yards out, leaving the Redmen chasing the game against a Red Star side who were a different proposition on their home turf.

Klopp brought on both Firmino and Divock Origi – for his first LFC appearance in 15 months – but Liverpool couldn't find a way through with Robertson and Salah hitting the woodwork and Matip missing a free header when he should have scored.

For Red Star it was a night that will go down in Belgrade folklore. For Liverpool it was a night to forget and one that left their qualification hopes in the balance.

"We gave them too many set-pieces," said Klopp. "They scored with a header after the corner. The second goal was out of the blue – we gave the ball away and that's not cool in a game like this, an atmosphere like this, a situation like this. You then have

Pavkov puts Red Star one-up from a corner

Standard
Chartered
LFC
10

to play your football in a negative mood."

Writing in *The Guardian*, journalist Andy Hunter noted: "The Marakana's reputation for passion, hostility and incessant noise proved no exaggeration, although Klopp rightly insisted it was no excuse for the performance Liverpool served up.

"It was a spectacular backdrop and Red Star responded in kind. Red Star's display befitted the backing they received."

If there was something positive to come from the trip, however, it was the birth of a song that would ring around grounds wherever Liverpool played for the remainder of the season.

LFC season-ticket holder Ben Stevenson had been watching a YouTube video of River Plate fans in Argentina singing a rousing song called *De la Mano del Muneco*.

It was the club's song of the season as their fans followed the team to glory in the 2018 Copa Libertadores. It also inspired a ditty in tribute to Reds no9 Roberto Firmino.

"Bobby deserved a song," Ben told liverpoolfc.com. "Most of the other lads had one, and Jürgen had asked for a Bobby one the previous season, so we just thought it was a bit of a laugh.

"The River Plate video was doing the rounds on social-media. A few of the lads kept singing it while we were there and I just came up with the words: 'Give the ball to Bobby then he will score'. A couple of the lads thought it was quite good and we just sat down in a bar and came up with the rest of it.

"We started singing it on the bus from the city-centre to the ground, a load of young lads at the back of the bus cottoned on to it, and it all got going from there. The videos started going round and we were like, no way – that's caught on.

"It's surreal, but it's a good song, and any song that gives the players an extra 10 per cent is a good thing."

The original lyrics differed slightly from the version that has been widely sung since Ben first came up with it in Belgrade, but it proved to be the song of the season for Liverpool FC supporters throughout 2018/19.

Late sub Origi fails to make an impact this time

Standard
CHAMPIONS LEAGUE
CHAMPIONS LEAGUE

GAZPROM

Standard
Chartered

Standard
Chartered

It doesn't always go your way,
but you live to fight another day

LFC
FIRMINO

Red Star keeper Milan Borjan celebrates victory

The 'Bobby song' was sung incessantly for minutes on-end during some games. It sounded great when in full flow, a rip-roaring tune for a top-class player, and admired by the man himself.

"I think the song the Liverpool fans have for me is great," he told the LFC matchday programme. "I love it and I always listen to it when the fans sing it. It motivates me more when I'm on the pitch because I think about my family and I also think about winning the games. I think it is amazing!"

The other game in Group C saw Napoli and PSG play out a 1-1 draw in Italy, a result which left Firmino and Liverpool in joint-top spot of an increasingly tight group.

Elsewhere Real Madrid scored five times in Plzen, while Tottenham kept their slim qualification hopes alive as they registered their first win of the tournament, coming from behind to beat PSV 2-1 at Wembley with Harry Kane scoring twice in the final 12 minutes, including an 89th-minute winner.

RED STAR BELGRADE 2
LIVERPOOL 0

Rajko Mitic Stadium - Group C Matchday Four
Tuesday 6 November 2018 - Kick-off 5.55pm
Goals: Pavkov (22, 29)

RED STAR (4-2-3-1):
Borjan, Stojkovic (Gobeljic 59), Savic (C), Degenek, Rodic, Krsticic (Jovicic 73), Jovancic, Srnic, Marin (Causic 64), Ben, Pavkov. Subs not used: Popovic, Babic, Stojilkovic, Simic. Booked: Marin.

LIVERPOOL (4-3-3):
Alisson, Alexander-Arnold (Gomez 46), Matip, Van Dijk, Robertson, Wijnaldum, Milner (C), Lallana (Origi 79), Salah, Sturridge (Firmino 46), Mane. Subs not used: Mignolet, Fabinho, Keita, Moreno. Booked: Lallana.

Attendance: 51,318. Referee: Antonio Mateu Lahoz.

mastercard
GAZPROM
pepsi
Santander
Enjoy Responsibly
SVP
PELOUSE
INTERDITE
PLEASE
KEEP OFF
THE GRASS

NISSAN
mastercard
Hotels.com
Santander

L.F.C.
11
11
L.F.C.
L.F.C.

Jürgen on pre-match press-conference duty and
Mo and Gini on the pitch ahead of kick-off v PSG

Liverpool's trip to an in-form Paris Saint-Germain in late November was always going to be tricky. PSG had won 15 and drawn five of their previous 20 Champions League group matches at Parc Des Princes, scored 28 goals in their last seven Champions League home games and won 14 consecutive cup competitions in France plus five of the last six league titles.

Ahead of the game in the French capital, Virgil van Dijk said the Reds would need to focus on playing their own game. "We want to win in Paris," he told the pre-match media gathering. "We're not going to go there for a draw – we're not going there for anything else other than trying to produce a good performance and trying to win the game.

"It's going to be unbelievably tough because they are still unbeaten in the league and haven't lost at home for a long time.

"I think personally we need to play our own game, try to put them under pressure and stop them from doing what they're good at, which is playing football."

The Reds were unable to do that in the opening 40 minutes of a game which saw PSG show their best and worst qualities – thrilling attacking football against a backdrop of infuriating histrionics.

"The number of interruptions in the game was not cool," Klopp said after the 2-1 defeat. "We have won the fair-play league twice in England but we looked like butchers when you see the yellow cards we had.

Standard Chartered

"It was clever of PSG, of Neymar – especially him – but a lot of players went down like it was serious and we were not that calm."

Alisson made some excellent interventions as PSG started like a maison en feu but was beaten by left-back Juan Bernat's deflected shot in the 13th minute before Neymar swept home a second from a lightning-quick counterattack led by Kylian Mbappe in the 37th minute.

By that point Italian midfielder Marco Verratti could arguably have been sent off for a shuddering high lunge on Gomez but was only shown a yellow card by Polish referee Szymon Marciniak. He also booked six Liverpool players and failed to clamp down on some theatrics from Neymar and his team-mates with the PSG physio arguably covering more ground than some of the players.

Indeed, when Mane was blatantly upended by Angel Di Maria in the box on the stroke of half-time the referee initially awarded a corner only to overrule himself after the official behind the goal had a word in his earpiece.

James Milner stepped up and confidently sent legendary goalkeeper Gianluigi Buffon the wrong way from the penalty-spot.

The goal gave Liverpool hope, but although they improved in the second half they never really came close to equalising as they lost a fourth successive away game in the competition for the first time in the club's history.

Daily Telegraph correspondent Chris Bascombe wrote: "The introduction of Naby Keita as substitute after an

Standard Chartered
10
14

Standard Chartered
5
MANÉ
10
VERRATTI
6
25

Neymar puts daylight between his team and the Reds on 37 minutes

LFC
LFC

hour – the player Liverpool hope will eventually add midfield variety – was the least surprising and most telling of the night.

"Keita's contribution was as encouraging as anything else in Paris. They need him fit and contributing."

Napoli's 3-1 home win over Red Star in the group's other game that evening left Liverpool with a slightly complex equation to ensure progress to the group stages.

The Reds now needed to beat Napoli 1-0 – or by two clear goals if the Italians scored – in their final Group C match to qualify.

Speaking to BT Sport post-match, captain Jordan Henderson said: "We're disappointed. We feel we're good enough to come here and win.

"It wasn't our night in the end but we tried to keep pushing for the equaliser.

"We kept going and kept fighting and now we just need to get through that game against Napoli at Anfield. It's still in our hands."

Liverpool versus Napoli under the lights a fortnight before Christmas. It was all set up for the kind of night Anfield comes alive for...

A second group-stage spot-kick for Milner but the Reds can't quite find an equaliser

“IT WASN’T OUR NIGHT BUT WE KEPT FIGHTING AND NOW WE JUST NEED TO GET THROUGH THAT GAME AGAINST NAPOLI AT ANFIELD – IT’S STILL IN OUR HANDS”

Fly
Emirates
14

HUBLOT

RESPECT

PARIS SAINT-GERMAIN 2
LIVERPOOL 1

Parc des Princes - Group C Matchday Five
Wednesday 28 November 2018 - Kick-off 8pm
Goals: Bernat (13), Neymar (37), Milner (45 pen)

PSG (4-2-3-1):
Buffon, Kehrer, Thiago Silva (C), Kimpembe, Bernat, Marquinhos, Verratti, Mbappe (Rabiot 85), Neymar, Di Maria (Dani Alves 65), Cavani (Choupo-Moting 65). Subs not used: Areola, Draxler, Diaby, Nsoki.
Booked: Verratti, Neymar.

LIVERPOOL (4-3-3):
Alisson, Gomez, Lovren, Van Dijk, Robertson, Milner (Shaqiri 77), Henderson (C), Wijnaldum (Keita 66), Salah, Firmino (Sturridge 71), Mane. Subs not used: Mignolet, Fabinho, Matip, Alexander-Arnold.
Booked: Wijnaldum, Gomez, Sturridge, Van Dijk, Robertson, Keita.

Attendance: 46,880. Referee: Szymon Marciniak.

MAKE OR BREAK IN THE
FINAL GROUP GAME…

L.F.C.
3

UEFA

adidas

The players training at Melwood in the evening to replicate match-night conditions

Standard Chartered
new balance
WESTERN UNION
BETVICTOR
LFC
BETVICTOR

BETVICTOR
L.F.C.

Anfield's date with destiny

3

Liverpool v Napoli

"Winning isn't everything – it's the only thing." Whether or not you agree with that quote attributed to legendary American Football coach Henry Russell Sanders, the Reds knew that it didn't necessarily apply to them in the context of their crucial Matchday Six encounter against Napoli at Anfield. In this case, winning might not mean anything.

In the build-up to the game on Tuesday 11 December, column inches were filled with the many and varied permutations. One-nil would be enough to see the Reds through to the knockout stages. But 2-1, 3-2 or even 4-3 would not be.

Another possible route to the last 16 was offered by a draw between Red Star and Paris Saint-Germain in Belgrade. Should that come to pass, then a Liverpool victory by any scoreline would see the Reds, Napoli and PSG all finish with nine points but Liverpool finish top of the group by virtue of having the best record among the three teams.

Jürgen Klopp did not want to be relying on others. As far as he and his side were concerned, one-nil or a victory by two clear goals was the required formula.

Both the Reds and their Italian visitors were in form, coming into the game on the back of 4-0 league wins the previous Saturday. While Liverpool were winning by that margin at Bournemouth courtesy of a Mohamed Salah hat-trick, Napoli were producing an impressive home victory over Frosinone in Serie A.

Their manager Carlo Ancelotti insisted that his side would adopt a similarly attacking approach in L4. "I have lots of memories of Anfield and my last one is a good one because I won the title there with Chelsea," he recalled.

"It's going to be a tough, exciting match. We'll go there and play our usual game. It would be counter-productive to try and 'park the bus'. Besides anything else, that's not how we play.

"We'll try to boss the game and I'm sure the lads are ready and fired up to give their absolute all. We'll go there with an attacking mindset."

From Liverpool's perspective, midfielder Fabinho was preparing himself for a European classic. "We know Napoli is an important game as it will decide our future in the competition," he said.

"Obviously we know all about them from playing in Naples. But it will be a boost having the fans with us at Anfield and we hope that we can win this game and get through to the next stage of the competition."

Two days before the fixture, a mural of Klopp appeared on a wall in the city's Baltic District, created by a graffiti artist over a two-day period especially for supporters to enjoy.

Twenty-four hours before the match the Reds received a boost when defender Joe Gomez signed a new long-term contract with the club. The 21-year-old England international explained: "Signing this new deal means the

The great Carlo Ancelotti in his pre-match press-call at Anfield

Young defender Joe Gomez commits his future to the Reds

world to me. I love the club, I love playing and learning here, and I am happy for that to continue."

As the countdown to kick-off continued, Klopp revealed it was no surprise to him that the outcome of Group C would prove to be so close.

In his programme notes he explained: "I always thought this group would come down to the final round of matches before we knew where our destiny would lie, so there is no sense of shock or surprise we face this challenge tonight.

"It has rightly been described as probably the toughest and most competitive group in the competition this season. PSG, Napoli and Red Star are outstandingly good teams and we are not too bad ourselves.

"Of course, I will not hide away from the fact that we face the situation we do because our performances and results away from home in the Champions League have not been to the high standards we hold ourselves to. If we earn the right to progress clearly it is something we will look to address. But we should also not ignore the fact that our future in the competition remains in our own hands, because we have been really good at Anfield.

"We all know what we have to do to qualify for the knockout stages. We won't be looking to Belgrade for help or assistance as it's completely irrelevant to us. We have a job to do – a game to win – and if we give our best I think we have a real opportunity. It's about this game.

"As much as we respect Napoli, I think tonight is about us and our potential, so that is where our focus will be entirely. As a club we live for moments like these.

"We know we have the quality, we know we have the mentality and we know we have the belief to do what is required. We are so blessed at Liverpool to have a dressing-room of players who embrace moments like these. They will relish being part of this occasion. They want to create their own memories and history – their own stories. They will look to make the night one of joy for our fans."

That's how it turned out, but not before Kopites had gone through the proverbial rollercoaster of emotions.

Winning 1-0 when you need to win 1-0 sounds simple enough, but Liverpool's victory to secure their place in the last 16 was far from straightforward. Famous European nights at Anfield wouldn't quite be the same without heart-stopping moments and the Reds getting the job done by the tightest of margins, which is precisely what happened here. Again.

Napoli needed a draw to progress and knew if they

NAPOLI
Kappa

Napoli's squad running through their drills as the boss looks on

scored Liverpool would need to win by two clear goals, so Ancelotti's side – beaten only by Juventus away from home all season – came to Anfield and had a go, which in turn gave the Reds some space to run into and exploit.

Virgil van Dijk was booked early on by Slovenian referee Damir Skomina for catching Belgian international forward Dries Mertens after winning the ball. Sadio Mane also had a goal disallowed before a moment of genius from Mohamed Salah unlocked the visitors' defence.

The *Guardian* sports writer Barney Ronay captured it perfectly: "Just past the half-hour at a chilly, angsty Anfield, Salah was suddenly free in space on the edge of the Napoli box, scampering in on goal in that bouncy style, hair flapping, legs whirring like a cartoon kangaroo.

"Salah clipped the ball hard and low past [goalkeeper] David Ospina without breaking stride. From a mix-and-match opening half-hour fraught with dead-ends Liverpool were 1-0 up: the game, the night, the group just about sliding their way.

"It was a significant moment in Salah's own drama, too. His focus has narrowed in recent weeks, his edge returned... Salah is good enough to be the Premier League's top scorer in mid-December.

"Here it always felt like Salah might make the difference on a breezy, finger-numbing night at Anfield. Ah, yes. Those Magical European Nights we hear so much about: sometimes a cliche is no less true for being a cliche. As ever the Kop was a shared pageantry of flags and banners, that single tier stretching right up into the eaves to create a noise-funnel effect the length of the pitch."

Knowing that one-nil would be enough, but also acutely aware that a Napoli goal would knock them out, the Reds worked, pressed and probed after the break but missed a plethora of chances – Salah, Mane, Gini Wijnaldum and Van Dijk the chief culprits – which meant the visitors were still in the game.

Then, in the 92nd minute, time seemed to stand still. Napoli launched one desperate last attack and the ball fell kindly to Arkadiusz Milik six yards out.

It was the type of moment that seems to take place in slow motion, the ramifications of what happens next whirling through the minds of everyone inside the stadium.

A Milik miss and the Reds could look forward to the round-of-16 draw the following week. A Milik goal and they'd be tucking into their Christmas turkey contemplating Thursday-night football in the Europa League.

YOU'LL NEVER WALK ALONE
LIVERPOOL
FOOTBALL CLUB
EST • 1892
UEFA CHAMPIONS LEAGUE
GROUP STAGE
LIVERPOOL FC
v SSC NAPOLI
ANFIELD STADIUM
11 DECEMBER 2018

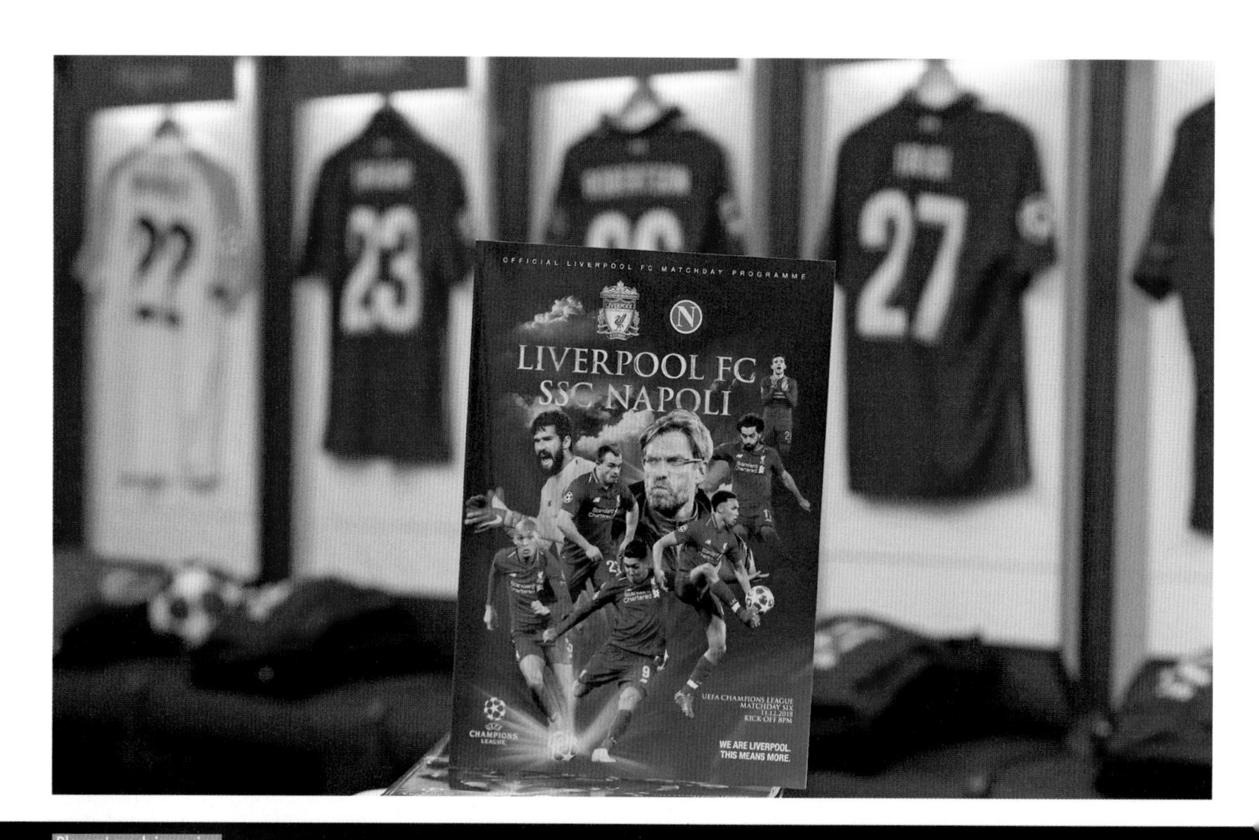

Players' coach incoming

The Polish striker seemed certain to score only for Alisson to fling himself forward and somehow block his shot, prompting chants of "Aaa-lisson! Aaa-lisson! Aaa-lisson!" around Anfield.

If people had raised eyebrows at the goalkeeper's high transfer fee earlier in the summer, they weren't doubting his quality now. Big players excel in big moments of big matches. And boy, had Alisson earned his corn.

Moments later the final whistle blew and Liverpool were through to the last 16 having made a raucous Anfield sweat it out, but then did you ever expect anything different?

In his own *Guardian* match report Daniel Taylor noted: "There is a reasonable theory that is how Anfield likes it best: under the floodlights, with the volume turned up and a kaleidoscope of banners on the Kop recalling the club's pedigree in Europe.

"For Liverpool, it was an examination of their temperament, as much as their skill, and they passed with distinction."

This was actually the first time that the Reds had progressed from a Champions League group having qualified automatically for it. They had previously been eliminated in seasons 2002/03, 09/10 and 14/15.

Andy Robertson was understandably delighted that he and his team had managed to end that statistical sequence. "We knew we had to get a fast start and that's what we did," he said after the final whistle.

"At nil-nil they had nothing to lose and they threw their centre-back forward.

"It was an unbelievable save from Alisson [to deny Milik]. But to get 1-0 up we were confident we would keep a clean sheet and thankfully that's what we did."

Robbo was later nominated for the Champions League player of the week award.

The Reds' no26 put in a typically relentless display from the left-back berth as he covered 10.83 kilometres during the course of the game and his efforts were subsequently recognised by UEFA, who on their official website pitted him against Neymar (Paris Saint-Germain away to Red Star), forward Guillaume Hoarau (Young Boys at home to Juventus) and eventual winner Leroy Sane (Manchester City versus Hoffenheim at the Etihad) for their Matchday Six performance prize.

The captain leads the team into the dressing-room

YNWA
YNWA
YNWA
26

YNWA
YNWA
YNWA
UEFA CHAMPIO
YOU'LL NEVER WALK ALONE
LIVERPOOL
FOOTBALL CLUB
EST·1892

LIVERPOOL FC
ALLEZ
BOSTON
CITY OF CHAMPIONS

LIVERPOOL
FOOTBALL CLUB
LIVERPOOL
LIVERPOOL

The following day's newspapers honed in on the contributions of Alisson and Salah. The *Liverpool Echo* carried the back-page headline 'Beck in business'. In its player ratings they described Alisson's stop as "one of the most remarkable saves you will ever see."

The Brazilian was awarded nine out of 10 for his contribution, as was Salah, who scored a "remarkable goal" and "looked a threat throughout the first half."

Echo correspondent James Pearce hailed Alisson's powers of concentration: "For most of the night the biggest danger to the Brazil international was frostbite as

Mo scores the all-important goal from the narrowest of angles

he stood and watched his side boss proceedings.

"But a combination of wasteful finishing and the heroics of David Ospina meant that Liverpool's Champions League fate remained in the balance."

The *Daily Mirror* went with 'Mo place like home' on its backpage, adding: "The only surprise was this remarkable player did not complement his first-half strike and head off the nervous finale Anfield had to endure."

Not surprisingly the Italian footballing press focused more on the shortcomings of Napoli rather than the heroics of the Reds.

The *Gazzetta dello Sport* front-page depicted a sea of sad faces, with both Napoli and Inter Milan being knocked out of the tournament on the same night. 'Salah-goal, regrets for Ancelotti' read their headline.

There was more despondency on the front page of *Corriere dello Sport* with the headline: 'Ci Rivediamo Giovedi' as in 'See you on Thursday' in reference to the Europa League.

There were, of course, contrasting emotions from the two managers. Ancelotti admitted: "We knew Liverpool were going to put us under a lot more pressure. The intensity was different compared to the first game against them. You can't expect to go to a place like Liverpool and create ten chances. Some of the players struggled to come to terms with the intensity of Liverpool.

"We're going out with our heads held extremely high. The players showed a great deal of character. There shouldn't be any regrets. It would have been a wonderful achievement to qualify. A lot of people weren't expecting

Lete

SALAH
11

No quarter given in a tense, engrossing encounter

us to take it to the last game. Perhaps we were missing that little bit of luck as well."

Klopp in contrast was beaming with delight: "It was unbelievable, what the boys did. I am still full of adrenaline about it. The boys played with their whole heart. Our offensive and defensive play and overall pressing was some of the best I ever saw. The intensity we played with was so difficult to deal with."

Asked about Alisson's brilliant late save, he added: "If I knew Alisson was this good, I would have paid double!"

Compliments were showered upon the Liverpool manager and his 'mentality monsters' after such a tough test against a side who would again go on to finish as runners-up in Serie A. One of the biggest came from BT Sport pundit Rio Ferdinand, the former Manchester United and England defender who was a Champions League winner in 2007/08.

"The tenacity with which Liverpool play is unrivalled in Europe at the moment," he said. "They are aggressive, on the front-foot and their attention to detail is something to behold, but when you've got Salah, Mane and Firmino backing it up you wouldn't want to play against them."

Contextualising the performance, *Echo* sports editor David Prentice felt the triumph was vindication of a more pragmatic approach put in place by Klopp. "The result was Liverpool's season in microcosm," he wrote. "The new controlled, disciplined Reds have supplanted the manic 'Boom! Boom! Boom!' Reds. After the 4-3s and the 5-2 of last season, this season has seen more measured, more moderate victories.

"There was an assumption pre-match that this would

The save that kept us in the Champions League… Alisson! Alisson! Alisson!

LOVREN
6
Standard
Chartered

MILIK
99

LOVREN
6
Standard Chartered

be another of 'those' European nights. Because when Liverpool need a European miracle, they usually produce one. St Etienne, Olympiakos, Borussia Dortmund...hell, even Auxerre. It's an illustrious roll call which has given some supporters a sense of misplaced confidence. As if Liverpool only have to turn up and Anfield only has to clear its throat for visiting defences to crumble. If only...

"Sometimes the controlled, disciplined single-goal successes are every bit as effective."

Liverpool and Napoli both finished with nine points but the Reds were placed second in the group because they matched the 1-0 win Napoli had achieved against them on Matchday Two and scored more goals in the group (nine) than the Italian side managed (seven).

Thomas Tuchel's team topped the group after winning 4-1 in Belgrade in a game which saw their front-three of Neymar, Edinson Cavani and Kylian Mbappe all score.

Liverpool's victory wasn't the only piece of drama in the final round of group games. Tottenham made it four English teams out of four in the last 16 when they went to the Nou Camp and drew 1-1 with Barcelona thanks to a late goal from Lucas Moura – something Spurs would call upon again later in the tournament. The two Manchester clubs had secured their qualification after Matchday Five.

Six days after Liverpool's victory, ex-Reds favourite Luis Garcia was in Nyon to help conduct the draw for the round of 16. Liverpool were paired with German giants Bayern Munich, meaning the first competitive meeting of the clubs since 2001 and the first in the European Cup/ Champions League since the semi-finals of 1981.

Klopp called it a "good draw. It was clear it would be difficult [and] they are obviously a top side. For me it's nice, going to Germany. But at the end it's a football game on the highest level and we have to play it.

"It's a tough one, but that's how it should be. It's the last 16 of the Champions League so there are only tough teams in and I'm really excited about it.

"So we have now time to prepare the game, a lot of time obviously, and hopefully we have all our players available then. It will be a tough one, an interesting one, and I am looking forward to it."

His side were settling into a nice rhythm and would go on to complete their punishing December schedule with a superb return of eight wins out of eight.

Top of the Premier League and with those February and March dates with Bayern lying in wait, there was a tangible sense of optimism in the air as Liverpool looked forward to what their 2019 would bring.

Napoli attacker Dries Mertens dejected at the end of the match

13

LIVERPOOL 1
NAPOLI 0

Anfield Group C - Matchday Six
Tuesday 11 December 2018 - Kick-off 8pm
Goal: Salah (34)

LIVERPOOL (4-3-3):
Alisson, Alexander-Arnold (Lovren 90), Matip, Van Dijk, Robertson, Wijnaldum, Henderson (C), Milner (Fabinho 85), Salah, Firmino (Keita 79), Mane. Subs not used: Mignolet, Sturridge, Shaqiri, Origi. Booked: van Dijk, Salah, Robertson, Mane.

NAPOLI (4-3-3):
Ospina, Maksimovic, Albiol, Koulibaly, Rui (Ghoulam 70), Allan, Hamsik (C), Ruiz (Zielinski 62), Callejon, Mertens (Milik 67), Insigne. Subs not used: Karnezis, Ounas, Hysaj, Diawara. Booked: Koulibaly.

Attendance: 52,015. Referee: Damir Skomina.

Lete
Lete
Standard Chartered
LFC
3
99

CHAMPIONS
LEAGUE

FABINHO
ALLAN
5
Standard Chartered

Standard
Chartered

So many heroes on the night and one extremely happy gaffer

Standard
Chartered
L.F.C.

11

LFC
L.F.C.
BETVICTOR
STEWARD
TV
064
PS4

“WHAT THE BOYS DID WAS UNBELIEVABLE AND I’M STILL FULL OF ADRENALINE – THEY PLAYED WITH THEIR HEARTS AND AN INTENSITY THAT WAS DIFFICULT TO LIVE WITH”

LIVERPOOL
YOU'LL NEVER
LIVERPOOL
YOU'LL NEVER WALK
VERPOOL v NAP
ENGLAND
11/12/2018
LIVERPOOL FC
YOU'LL NEVER WALK ALONE
LIVERPOOL FC
NEVER WALK ALONE
LIVERPOOL FC
NEVER WALK ALONE
Standard Chartered
VER POOL FC
NEVER WALK ALONE

YOU'LL NEVER WALK ALONE
LIVERPOOL FC
VAN DIJK
LIVERPOOL FC
YOU'LL NEVER WALK ALONE
LIVERPOOL FC
SSC NAPOLI
LIVERPOOL FC
YOU'LL NEVER WALK ALONE
LIVERPOOL FC
YOU'LL NEVER WALK ALONE
THE FA CUP SEMI FINAL 2012
SATURDAY 14TH APRIL 2012 · WEMBLEY STADIUM
LIVERPOOL FC
UEFA CHAMPIONS LEAGUE 2018-19
LIVERPOOL FC
YOU'LL NEVER WALK ALONE
ALLEZ ALLEZ

What would the knockout rounds hold in store for Mo and the boys?

11

ROUND OF 16 AND THE QUARTER-FINALS...

L.F.C.
4

Grey skies over Melwood as the players prepare for the following night's first leg with Bayern at Anfield

Standard Chartered

liverpoolfc.com
liverpoolfc.com

24

Old adversaries

Liverpool v Bayern Munich, Bayern Munich v Liverpool
Liverpool v FC Porto, FC Porto v Liverpool

Ten European Cups: 1974, 1975, 1976, 1977, 1978, 1981, 1984, 2001, 2005 and 2013. Five apiece. Plus a combined 46 domestic league titles.

If Liverpool versus Bayern Munich sounded like a big game when the draw for the last 16 was made it's because it is a *grosses spiel*, as they say in Germany. A proper heavyweight clash between European royalty yet the first in the Champions League since the 1981 European Cup semi-final.

Perhaps that 38-year absence made the prospect of the two sides meeting all the more mouthwatering, but then two-and-a-half months is a long time between drinks in football.

A lot had happened, both on and off the pitch, and between Liverpool's 1-0 victory against Napoli and the first leg of the Champions League last 16 clash with FCB at Anfield ten weeks later.

Peter Thompson, Liverpool legend and a dazzling winger with "balance like a ballet dancer" according to Bill Shankly, passed away on New Year's Eve 2018 at the age of 76. Auld acquaintances are never forgotten at Anfield.

Squad players Dominic Solanke and Lazar Markovic moved on to pastures new (Bournemouth and Fulham respectively) when the January transfer-window was ajar, Mo Salah was named as CAF African player of the year – again – while Liverpool Football Club announced a record profit of £106m.

On the pitch it was even busier. Jürgen Klopp's side played 11 games – ten of them in the Premier League plus a televised FA Cup third-round defeat at Wolverhampton Wanderers – between Napoli's dismissal and Bayern's arrival in the next stage of the Champions League.

Results were on the good side of mixed, the weather on the mixed side of bad.

Wins against Manchester United, Wolves, Newcastle United, Arsenal, Brighton & Hove Albion, Crystal Palace and Bournemouth were all chalked up, but draws against Leicester City at a snowy Anfield and down at West Ham,

plus a 2-1 defeat at Manchester City – the Reds' first in the league all season – made for a compelling title race.

Liverpool led rivals City by one point on the day of the Napoli game (11 December). By the time Bayern arrived on Merseyside (19 February), City led on goal-difference, having played a game more.

During that ten-week period the Reds had built up and lost a seven-point lead, but the final Premier League table would show that City's win at the Etihad – Liverpool's only defeat in the league all season – would prove to be the decisive result during a relentless race to the finish that ended with the Mancunians on 98 points and the Liverpudlians on 97. Not that anybody knew what was to come in mid-February.

A rare gap in the fixture-list allowed Klopp to take his players to Marbella to prepare for the first leg against Bayern, the Reds playing at Anfield first due to being group-stage runners-up. The manager had a problem to solve.

Virgil van Dijk, the towering foundation on which Liverpool's defensive strength was built, was suspended. He received just one yellow card in 38 Premier League games, but three in six Champions League group games was enough to rule him out of the next fixture in the tournament.

To compound VVD's loss, Dejan Lovren and Joe Gomez were both injured while Trent Alexander-Arnold was only just returning from injury. Fabinho had been forced to play a couple of games at centre-half, both James Milner and Jordan Henderson had deputised at

Jürgen facing a familiar foe from Germany

CHAMPIONS LEAGUE
MADRID 19
FINAL
OFFICIAL MATCH BALL
adidas
LIVERPOOL FC
v FC Bayern München
74
75
76
77
78
81
84
01
05
13

RESPECT

RESPECT

Nobody could take their eyes or lenses off proceedings

right-back, but this came in games when Van Dijk had been playing.

How would Liverpool cope without him against a Bayern Munich side that'd won six consecutive Bundesliga titles, reached at least the Champions League quarter-final for six years in a row and scored in every away game, bar one, in which they had played during 2018/19?

"We need to be full-throttle for that game," said left-back Andy Robertson. "They are such a good team and they have been the last six or seven years, so we know what a tough task it will be. But we believe we can cause any teams problems and we have to be at our best."

Captain Henderson, writing in his official matchday programme notes, gave a rallying call that *Game of Thrones*' Jon Snow would've been proud of.

"Bayern are a team of winners – winning is in their DNA as a club. They're a club who are used to being successful domestically and more often than not are always involved in the Champions League's very latter stages, so when this competition starts each season they'll fancy themselves as potential winners of it.

"They're a squad packed with experience and top quality, a club whom we have the utmost respect for. We know how tough a challenge they will pose over these two legs. But I think we made a statement in the last campaign about what the European Cup means to us and how we don't bend the knee to anyone else in it."

Elbows may have been bent by the thousands of Bayern fans who enjoyed themselves in Liverpool city-centre on the afternoon of the match before marching up Scotland Road and Everton Valley to Anfield, but nobody in a red shirt was bending the knee when the game kicked off.

Liverpool not only kept a clean-sheet against Bayern Munich but prevented them from even having a shot on target. And while the Reds struggled to create opportunities at the other end, with Bayern's aim of getting a draw at Anfield best exemplified by full-backs Joshua Kimmich and David Alaba maintaining their defensive positions instead of flying forward at full-pelt as they usually do, nil-nil wasn't the worst result in a two-legged tie that could be settled on away-goals.

Fabinho deputised brilliantly for the suspended Van Dijk at centre-half alongside Joel Matip – who came closest to scoring for the visitors when Alisson had to save his miscued clearance – and with midfielders Henderson, Javi Martinez and Bayern centre-back Mats Hummels the three best players on the pitch, it was no wonder chances were at a premium.

A tough, physical first-leg encounter yields no goals

Standard
Chartered
adidas
22
6

Mo Salah saw Manuel Neuer clutch his flicked volley early on and put a header wide of the target, but the best chance fell to Sadio Mane in the 33rd minute after Naby Keita's effort deflected to him. With his back to goal he shot on the turn but dragged the ball past the far post.

Mane also saw a spectacular overhead-kick fly wide before Matip could only fire a first-time shot, from Roberto Firmino's pass, past the post in an opening half that was far more exciting than the second. The only real chance of note was a late Mane diving header that Neuer pushed around the post while at the other end Alisson could've spent most of the 45 minutes playing *Allez Allez Allez* on his guitar, having been filmed by LFCTV in session with BOSS Night's Jamie Webster in the city's Baltic Triangle district ahead of the game.

"There is a lesson in Bayern's approach, the consequences of which Liverpool may encounter more often now that Klopp has re-established the club's reputation," wrote Chris Bascombe in the *Daily Telegraph*. "Visitors know what to expect on a European night now. Liverpool will have to continue to raise their game to live up to their European reputation."

The German press concluded it was a good result for Bayern, but while many Kopites left Anfield disappointed not to see a Liverpool win, they also knew it would be a very different game at the Allianz Arena where Bayern are obliged to attack. And they were right.

Bayern keeper Neuer and his defence keep the Reds at bay

LIVERPOOL 0
BAYERN MUNICH 0

Anfield - Round of 16 first leg
Tuesday 19 February 2019 - Kick-off 8pm

LIVERPOOL (4-3-3):
Alisson, Alexander-Arnold, Matip, Fabinho, Robertson, Wijnaldum, Henderson (C), Keita (Milner 76), Salah, Firmino (Origi 76), Mane. Subs not used: Mignolet, Sturridge, Moreno, Lallana, Shaqiri. Booked: Henderson.

BAYERN MUNICH (4-3-3):
Neuer (C), Kimmich, Süle, Hummels, Alaba, Thiago, Martinez, Rodriguez (Renato Sanches 88), Gnabry (Rafinha 90), Lewandowski, Coman (Ribery 81). Subs not used: Ullreich, Davies, Mai, Shabani. Booked: Kimmich.

Attendance: 52,250. Referee: Gianluca Roccho.

Alisson's turn to field the questions in the pre-match press conference for the return leg in Munich

L.F.C

A spectacular light show before the game kicks off in the Allianz

We had to wait 22 days, though. The opening round of knockout fixtures in the Champions League is held over a four-week period rather than a fortnight. So over three weeks had elapsed before the two sides reconvened in Munich.

Liverpool had never played a competitive fixture at the Allianz before, Bayern's former Olympiastadion home hosting the last meeting of the two clubs in 1981. But the Reds had visited the Allianz to play in the pre-season Audi Cup tournament back in August 2017.

Back then a huge away-following went with them, meaning that the travelling Kop already knew Munich pretty well.

Kilians Irish Pub on Frauenplatz, a minute's walk from Munich's Marienplatz – the city's historic central square – was a meeting-point for many. But the Marienplatz was red.

Liverpool flags hung from seemingly every parasol, protecting patrons of the local bars from the wintry conditions, around the square. 'WHEN LIVERPOOL WIN WE ALL WIN' read one. 'SCOUSERS ALL OVER THE WORLD' said another.

Underneath those giant umbrellas, *steins* full of local *braus* such as Spaten and Augustiner were keeping throats well-lubricated as song after song was bellowed out.

Across town, close to Hirschgarten – home of the biggest beer-garden in Munich and possibly the world, with seating for 8,000 customers – a first-ever BOSS Night session on tour was held at Backstage on Reitknechtstrasse.

Free to enter, and with Scouse musicians Jamie Webster and Kieran Molyneux calling the tunes, the place rocked to the Liverpool soundtrack, but as the evening drew on all *strasses* led to the Allianz.

Situated next to an autobahn on the northern outskirts of Munich, a ten-minute walk from Frottmanning U-Bahn station the Allianz looks like a giant airship that has landed on a hill in the middle of nowhere.

The unusual foil-air panelling on the exterior and the sheer size of the venue gives the Allianz an alluring quality. At night the luminous exterior beams out red and white lights, piercing the darkness. Bayern Munich's stadium glows.

Inside the ground, with three tiers designed in a bowl shape and seats far closer to the pitch than in their previous home, the Allianz has a bit of Wembley, a touch

He's turned, he's spun, and now Sadio Mane is about to float the ball into the Bayern net

L.F.C.
Standard
Chartered

of the Emirates and a sense of Cardiff's Principality Stadium about it. It also had 4,000 travelling Kopites inside it on the night of 13 March 2019.

Klopp, who was preparing for his 24th match against Bayern during his managerial career, was asked in the pre-match press-conference about what kind of atmosphere he expected his side to face at the 70,000-capacity stadium?

"To our Liverpool fans I would say don't hesitate and give it your all. You can be loud, you can influence. The atmosphere is good here, actually, to be honest. It will be good tomorrow.

"There is only one chance to calm it down and that's with football – as well, I think we should give it a try. But it will be difficult, it is a good place to come, it is a good place to enjoy football. It is a good atmosphere, close and all that stuff [which] makes a difference. So there is nothing between us and a good football game, so let's enjoy it, let's try."

It proved to be a fantastic night, one of the best in Liverpool's illustrious European story, and an occasion when Liverpool created a piece of history. Bayern's Bavarian motto – *Mia san mia* – translates as 'We are who we are', but it was Klopp's Liverpool who showed who they are at the Allianz: potential Champions League winners.

Camp Nou? Check. San Siro? Check. Santiago Bernabeu? Check. And now the Allianz Arena could be

Van Dijk's towering header puts Liverpool back in front - with more to come

ticked off an exclusive list thanks to a statement-making 3-1 Liverpool win. No English team had ever won at all four cathedrals of European football before, but the Reds completed the collection in style and were full value for their win.

The return of Van Dijk – the footballing equivalent of having your boiler back on after a day without it in the middle of winter – was a boost. But Liverpool suffered an early injury blow when Henderson was forced off in the 13th minute with a twisted ankle. On came Fabinho, in his preferred midfield role, but it was Van Dijk and Mane who were the game-changers.

Kimmich, Bayern's usual right-back, was suspended after being booked at Anfield. His replacement, Brazilian Rafinha, couldn't cope with Mane's movement and pace.

With 26 minutes on the clock, the game seemingly in a lull with the ball at Van Dijk's feet, he spotted Mane about to make a darting run inside Rafinha. Ping. The ball dropped effortlessly into Mane's path as he sprinted forward, but goalkeeper Manuel Neuer – a giant presence of a man dressed all in blue – had spotted the intention and rushed out towards him. What happened next was world-class.

Mane, with one touch of his outstep while on the run, controlled the ball brilliantly before he swivelled past the onrushing keeper with another touch that left Neuer stumbling in the opposite direction, as if a runaway dog he was trying to catch had sold him a dummy.

Standard
Chartered

Mane nods home from
Mo's marvellous cross

In the blink of an eye, as Rafinha and Hummels tried to get back to protect their goal, Mane clipped a left-footed shot beyond them that spun in the air and dropped into the net.

"What a touch this is!" exclaimed BT Sport co-commentator Steve McManaman, formerly of this parish. "A real moment of class from Sadio Mane and Liverpool are 1-0 up away from home."

Klopp celebrated on the touchline by looking up towards the travelling Liverpool supporters, swirling his fist four times in the air before unleashing a full-strength fist-pump, like he'd been winding his arm up to gain power before releasing it skywards.

It was almost as if he knew Mane's goal would be decisive. And it was.

At no stage did Bayern ever lead the tie. They did force an equaliser before the break when Serge Gnabry evaded the offside trap and sent in a low cross that Matip could only turn into his own net while trying to stop Robert Lewandowski from scoring. But after the interval the Reds showed just what a good away European team they can be in knockout football.

Salah stung Neuer's gloves with a fizzing effort before Alexander-Arnold almost scored directly from a corner, the Bayern captain clawing the ball away from underneath his crossbar as Matip tried to get his head on it.

Milner trotted over to take the resultant corner from

L.F.C.

the other side and put it right onto Van Dijk's head, seven yards from goal. Hummels tried to challenge the big Dutchman, but it was no contest as he powered a downward header past Neuer's grasping glove. Sixty-nine minutes played, but game pretty much over.

A second goal from Mane with six minutes to play, another downward header from Salah's precise cross and his ninth Champions League knockout-stage goal, added a touch of gloss to the scoreline as Liverpudlian voices echoed around the emptying Allianz Arena.

Indeed, when the travelling Kop eventually left their seats high up in the gods after the full-time whistle peeped, they continued to incessantly sing the new Bobby Firmino *Si Senor* chant in the concourse, on the stairwells, outside the Allianz and on the Munich metro back into the city-centre. And why wouldn't they?

Not only had the Redmen booked their place in another Champions League quarter-final, they'd completed an awesome foursome of winning at Camp Nou, the San Siro, Santiago Bernabeu and now the Allianz in the space of 13 seasons.

"The boys love the competition, they really dig in in these moments," beamed Klopp afterwards. "The attitude was outstanding. The front-three were outstanding, the boys who came on helped a lot.

"We've laid down a marker tonight that LFC is back on the top level of European football."

Triumph for the manager but magnanimity in victory too

BAYERN MUNICH 1
LIVERPOOL 3

Allianz Arena - Round of 16 second leg
Wednesday 13 March 2019 - Kick-off 8pm
Goals: Mane (26, 84), Matip (39 og), Van Dijk (69)

BAYERN MUNICH (4-2-3-1):
Neuer (C), Rafinha, Süle, Hummels, Alaba, Martinez (Goretzka 72), Thiago, Gnabry, Rodriguez (Renato Sanches 79), Ribery (Coman 61), Lewandowski. Subs not used: Ulreich, Boateng, Davies, Jeong. Booked: Thiago, Renato Sanches.

LIVERPOOL (4-3-3):
Alisson, Alexander-Arnold, Matip, Van Dijk, Robertson, Wijnaldum, Henderson (C) (Fabinho 13), Milner (Lallana 87), Salah, Firmino (Origi 83), Mane. Subs not used: Mignolet, Lovren, Sturridge, Shaqiri. Booked: Fabinho, Matip, Robertson.

Attendance: 68,145. Referee: Daniele Orsato.

Eleven years ago, in February 2008, Brazilian goalkeeper Julio Cesar found himself picking the ball out of the net at Anfield twice. He was keeping goal for Internazionale at the time, but couldn't stop Dirk Kuyt and Steven Gerrard from scoring late goals to give Liverpool a 2-0 win in the first leg of the Champions League last 16. Three weeks later Fernando Torres also beat him with the only goal as the Redmen won at the San Siro.

A little over a decade on, Julio Cesar again found himself picking out a Liverpool ball, but this time he was on a stage in Nyon, in a lecture theatre at UEFA headquarters, conducting the draw for the 2018/19 Champions League quarter-final.

It's always a nervy time waiting for Liverpool to be drawn out of UEFA's plastic pots. Endless possibilities go through your mind of who you'd like to draw, who you want to avoid and whether the Reds will play at Anfield first or second. Lives are arranged around fixtures.

The seemingly endless pre-amble before the draw itself actually takes place adds frustration to the anticipation and even when the plastic balls, designed like Kinder Surprise eggs with Champions League branding replacing the chocolate, are pulled out, there's still a wait while they are unscrewed. Trying to catch a glimpse of the name on the paper inside in the two seconds before it is unfolded is all part of the dance.

Julio Cesar picked out Ajax first. Then Juventus. Next out? Liverpool. The Reds would play at Anfield first and, given that Manchester City, Manchester United and Tottenham Hotspur were still in the pot, alongside Barcelona and Porto, an English opponent seemed inevitable. Wrong.

"Liverpool FC will play...FC Porto," announced UEFA's Giorgio Marchetti after Julio Cesar unscrewed the Portuguese side's ball. "Yes Julio, we have completed 50 per cent of the job." Although that wasn't strictly true.

The road to Madrid was mapped out with the semi-final also drawn, pitting the winners of Liverpool v Porto against the winners of Manchester United v Barcelona. The general feeling among Kopites was Liverpool had a good draw.

The Reds had met Porto en route to Kiev in 2018 and, quite frankly, dismantled them in the first leg at Estadio do Dragao with a Sadio Mane hat-trick helping to condemn the twice Champions of Europe to a 5-0 defeat on a night when the travelling Kop introduced *Allez Allez Allez* to their repertoire.

OFFICIAL LIVERPOOL FC MATCHDAY PROGRAMME
LIVERPOOL FC
CHAMPIONS LEAGUE
QUARTER-FINAL FIRST LEG
09.04.2019
KICK-OFF 8PM
FC PORTO
WE ARE LIVERPOOL. THIS MEANS MORE.
CHAMPIONS LEAGUE
MADRID 19
FINAL
OFFICIAL MATCH BALL
adidas

NISSAN

"IT'S OFF TO THE MATCH WE GO"

Whichever way you look at it,
Keita's opener was crucial

Porto would come to Anfield first this time. The Reds' young Portuguese winger Rafa Camacho pointed out in the matchday programme that "they are a totally different team to when we played them last year." But there was an air of confidence amongst Liverpudlians that they could and would be beaten. It was well-founded confidence.

On the Friday night before Porto visited Anfield, midfielder Naby Keita had scored his first Liverpool goal, the equaliser in a 3-1 Premier League win at Southampton. It was a weight off the Guinea international's shoulders as the longer he'd gone without scoring, the more questions were being asked about his value to the team following his summer arrival from RB Leipzig.

It proved to be a goalscoring catalyst for him as, like a 10A bus on Prescot Road, you wait ages for one and then two come along at once. Naby would also break the deadlock against Porto.

Anfield expected a win. You could sense it in the stadium. Last season's 5-0 aggregate victory – the second leg was a 0-0 dead-rubber – was a contributory factor, but so too were the facts that Porto had never beaten the Reds and had also lost 16 and drawn three of their previous 19 away European games in England.

Factor-in Klopp's unbeaten home record at Anfield in European competition and the belief Liverpool supporters have in him and his team, and it felt like there could only be one result. Once again, the Redmen delivered.

Milner came in at left-back for the suspended Robertson and Keita retained his spot in midfield. Just five minutes after kick-off he had his first Anfield goal when he received a pass from Firmino, fired goalwards and watched the ball spin past Iker Casillas after it deflected off the boot of Oliver Torres.

"I really enjoyed that moment against Porto," he later reflected. "It felt great to score my first goal at Anfield, but more than anything it gave me even more desire to do well and to win that game.

"It was a confidence boost as well, a big positive for my confidence, but I also think it helped the team in that moment. It gave the team more belief that we could score more goals against Porto and get through the tie."

It put Liverpool in control and the decision to play Henderson in a more advanced midfield position paid off 21 minutes later after Salah had clipped a shot agonisingly wide. The captain's perfectly-weighted pass played in Alexander-Arnold down the right and he

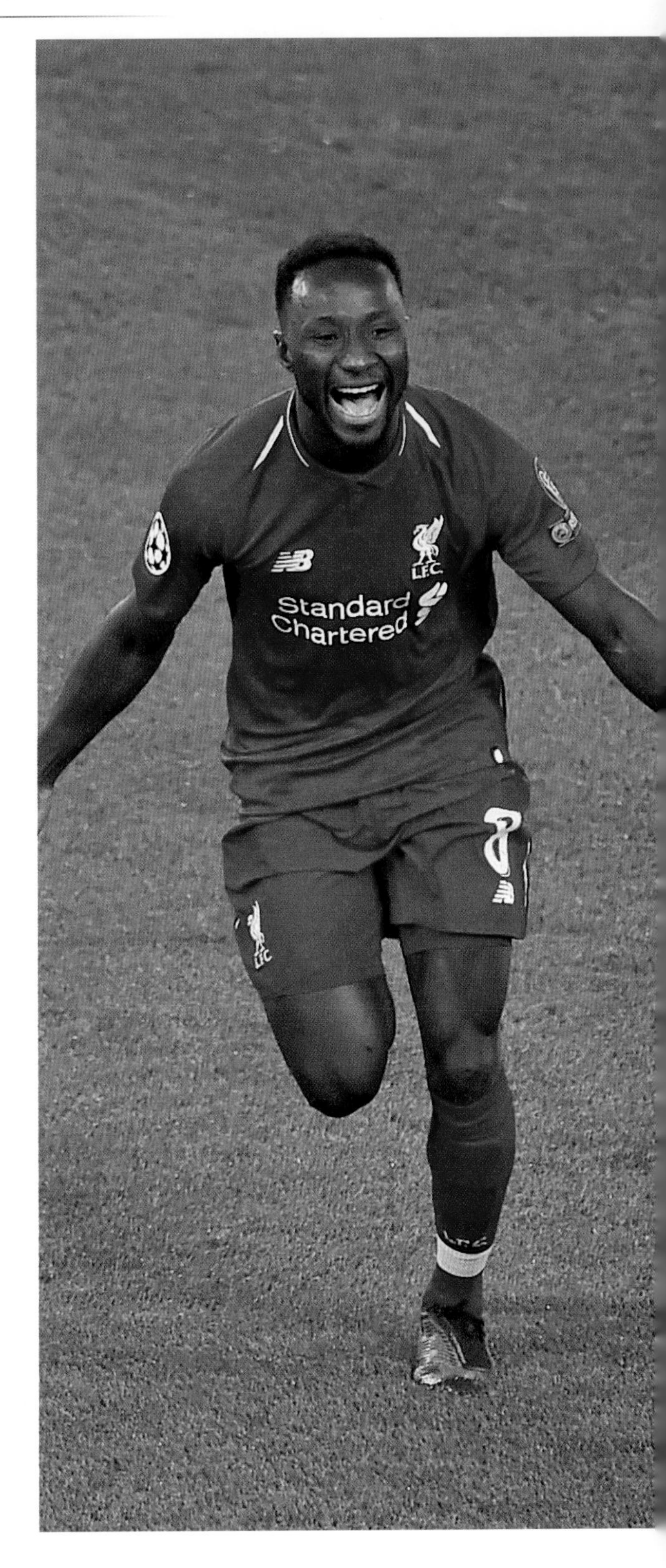

Bobby passes no2 into the Porto net
- and he's looking this time, too!

Job done… so far

centred the ball for Firmino to tap in at the far post. It was Bobby's 14th goal in the Champions League for LFC – only Steven Gerrard has scored more.

Porto did have their chances but Moussa Marega wasted all three of them, shooting straight at Alisson twice and blazing another shot over. They also had two penalty claims for handball against Alexander-Arnold and Dejan Lovren sent to VAR with stadium announcer George Sephton's confirmation that neither were penalties loudly cheered.

Mane had a goal ruled out for offside by both the assistant-referee and VAR, but with a two-goal advantage to take to northwest Portugal and no away-goals conceded by Alisson, the Reds could head there with one boot in the semi-final.

"We've taken the first step," said Firmino afterwards. "We played well and we scored goals. Now we have to keep our feet on the ground because the next game will be difficult as well.

"We have to give it our all away at their stadium."

LIVERPOOL 2
FC PORTO 0

Anfield - Quarter-final first leg
Tuesday 9 April 2019 - Kick-off 8pm
Goals: Keita (5), Firmino (26)

LIVERPOOL (4-3-3):
Alisson, Alexander-Arnold, Lovren, Van Dijk, Milner, Henderson (C), Fabinho, Keita, Salah, Firmino (Sturridge 82), Mane (Origi 73). Subs not used: Mignolet, Wijnaldum, Gomez, Shaqiri, Matip.

FC PORTO (4-4-2):
Casillas, Maxi Pereira (Fernando 77), Felipe, Militao, Telles, Corona, Danilo (C), Torres (Bruno Costa 73), Marega, Soares (Brahimi 62). Subs not used: Vana, Leite, Hernani, Andre Pereira. Booked: Soares, Felipe.

Attendance: 52,465. Referee: Antonio Mateu Lahoz.

GIVE
FC Porto
A VENCER DESDE 1893
PORTO
F.C.Porto
C. PORTO

Porto is one of Europe's oldest cities. It may not be quite as large as Lisbon, home of FC Porto's biggest rivals Benfica and Sporting Club de Portugal, but in 1996 UNESCO proclaimed its 'historical core' as a World Heritage Site.

Five years later Gerard Houllier's Liverpool side visited Porto for the first time in unusual circumstances. The Reds were there for a UEFA Cup quarter-final, but Houllier, his players and Liverpool supporters had to walk through trays of disinfectant on arrival at the airport to help prevent the spread of the foot-and-mouth outbreak that had engulfed the UK.

The goalless draw that followed, at Porto's former Estadio Das Antas home, was a far cry from what was to come at Estadio do Dragao in 2019 and vice-captain Milner explained the sense of belief in the Liverpool camp during the pre-match press conference.

"I think there's a confidence within the squad and not an over-confidence, which is important," he said. "But you're never going to play a full season playing your best football, and I think that's the most important thing to remember.

"In long seasons when you're pushing for trophies, league titles and Champions Leagues, it's the tricky 15, 20 minutes, the 45 minutes where you're not on your game – can you keep a clean-sheet, can you regroup and can you push forward and get a result? We've managed to do that at tough times and hopefully that continues."

It was almost as if Milner had pre-empted how Porto would approach the second leg – the Dragons came out full of fire and brimstone, but not before manager Sergio Conceicao tried to butter the Reds up.

"Liverpool give me all what I like about football," he said. "In terms of their players and the way they play in the game. I like the Liverpool dynamics. I like the Liverpool game model. I like the way they play and the way they are with the ball – and also without it.

"It is similar to how I see football and in a lot of these moments in a game, they are the best team in the world."

High praise indeed, but Klopp wasn't about to let it get to his players' heads and create even a sniff of complacency: "We're not here to celebrate our situation – we are here to go to the next round. My players are not silly, they do not underestimate things like this. Porto are a good team."

Between the two games Liverpool lost another legend. Tommy Smith, the 'Anfield Iron' who Bill Shankly

Pro

I. CASILLAS
7
Pro

Mane slides home the first goal then Salah finishes off a breakneck counter-attack

famously said "wasn't born, he was quarried" and who captained the Reds to a league and UEFA Cup double in 1973, passed away at the age of 74. He made 638 appearances for the club and probably six times as many tackles.

Smithy famously scored for Liverpool in the 1977 European Cup final in Rome, but to get to Madrid 2019 a job still needed doing in Porto. Around 2,500 travelling Kopites – one or two who had perhaps sampled the local vinho – took their places high up in Estadio do Dragao, where it always seems to rain. They saw another emphatic Liverpool win, this time 4-1.

"Although we're an attacking team we're very good at protecting ourselves too – teamwork is one of our biggest strengths," said Fabinho in an earlier LFC matchday programme, his own progression during his impressive debut campaign mirroring that of the Reds' displays on the road to Madrid.

Indeed, it was a measure of how far Liverpool have come under Klopp that they became the first English side to reach consecutive Champions League semi-finals in a decade, having not even been in European competition in 2016/17.

Furthermore, this 4-1 victory was ultimately so comfortable that the Reds looked like they had a couple of extra gears to use if needed. Perhaps Conceicao meant what he had said after all. He must certainly be sick of the sight of Liverpool after another drubbing in his own backyard.

Porto started well. Very well. They fired 14 shots on goal in the opening 20 minutes, but with Marega again forgetting his shooting boots Alisson was hardly stretched to keep them out before the Reds took the lead in the 26th minute.

“ALTHOUGH WE’RE AN ATTACKING TEAM WE’RE VERY GOOD AT PROTECTING OURSELVES TOO – TEAMWORK IS ONE OF OUR BIGGEST STRENGTHS”

L.F.C.
Standard
Chartered
3

76:31
1:2
MILITÃO
SALAH
LFC
9
GAZPROM

GAZPROM

Van Dijk nods home to make it four for the Reds in the Dragons' Den and 6-1 on aggregate

Mane was initially denied by the offside flag when he turned Salah's cross into the net, but VAR – fast-tracked for the Champions League knockout stages after originally being planned for 2019/20 – intervened.

A review showed that the Senegalese striker was onside and the goal was given. There was no way back for Porto after that.

Salah had appeared on the front cover of *Time* magazine a few days earlier, named as one of the 100 most influential people in the world. "Mo Salah is a better human being than he is a football player. And he's one of the best football players in the world," proclaimed comedian and Reds fan John Oliver.

"Mo is an iconic figure for Egyptians, Scousers and Muslims the world over, and yet he always comes across as a humble, thoughtful, funny man who isn't taking any of this too seriously.

"As a footballer, he plays with an infectious joy. I've always wondered what it would feel like to be able to play as well as him, and watching his face light up after he does something incredible, you get the reassuring sense that it's exactly as fun as you'd want it to be. I absolutely love him."

The Egyptian King's influence on the Liverpool team has never been in doubt and in the 65th minute Salah made it 2-0, clinically slotting the ball past Casillas when Alexander-Arnold played him clean through.

A minute later there was cause for further celebration when Joe Gomez made a welcome return from injury, coming on as a substitute for his first appearance since being injured during a 3-1 win at Burnley on the first midweek of December.

An Eder Militao header from a corner gave Porto a goal back, prompting the home fans on Curva Super Dragoes behind the goal to wave their giant blue-and-white flags with a tad more frenzy.

But Liverpool's two other substitutes soon combined to make it 3-1, Firmino heading Henderson's cross into the net.

Up in the away-end the Liverpool supporters were having a right old sing-song and as Milner prepared to take an 84th-minute corner the Virgil van Dijk song was ringing out. "He'll pass the ball, calm as you like, he's Virgil van Dijk, he's..." GOAL!

At the precise moment they were singing his name, Virgil nodded the ball into the net after Mane flicked Milner's corner on. Porto 1 Liverpool 4.

Now for Barcelona.

Standard Chartered
Standard Chartered
Standard Chartered
LFC
14
L.F.C.

FC PORTO 1
LIVERPOOL 4

Estadio do Dragao - Quarter-final second leg
Wednesday 17 April 2019 - Kick-off 8pm
Goals: Mane (26), Salah (65), Militao (68), Firmino (77), Van Dijk (84)

FC PORTO (4-3-3):
Casillas, Militao, Pepe, Felipe, Telles, Otavio (Soares 46), Danilo, Herrera (C), Corona (Fernando 78), Marega, Brahimi (Bruno Costa 81). Subs not used: Vana, Maxi Pereira, Torres, Andre Pereira. Booked: Pepe.

LIVERPOOL (4-3-3):
Alisson, Alexander-Arnold (Gomez 66), Van Dijk, Matip, Robertson (Henderson 71), Wijnaldum, Fabinho, Milner (C), Salah, Mane, Origi (Firmino 77). Subs not used: Mignolet, Keita, Sturridge, Shaqiri. Booked: Mane.

Attendance: 49,117. Referee: Danny Makkelie.

"THIS TEAM NEVER STOPS, THIS TEAM NEVER QUITS..."

L.F.C.
5

FCB

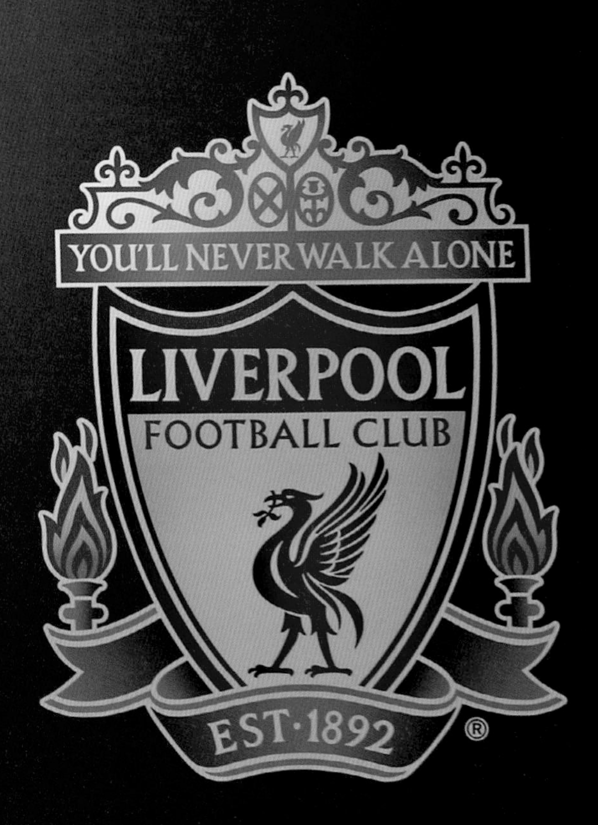

2019

NOU

L.F.C.

The semi-final

5

Barcelona v Liverpool
Liverpool v Barcelona

FC Barcelona. *Mes que un club.* Spanish champions with three games to spare. Copa del Rey finalists. Unbeaten in the Champions League. And with Lionel Messi – 46-goal Lionel Messi – targeting the European Cup, having seen Real Madrid win three in a row.

"We will do everything possible so that beautiful and desired cup returns here to Camp Nou," he said at a pre-season friendly against Boca Juniors in August, after being named as club captain following the departure of Andres Iniesta to Japan.

Messi reiterated his aim at Christmas in an interview with Marca – "The Champions League is always special for what it means and we would like to win it again, we have that dream" – before going on to speak of Barça's main rivals for the trophy.

"I know the PSG players because I follow the French League. Juve are very strong and with Cristiano there, even more so. [Manchester] City play very colourful football. Bayern have risen again. It's very difficult to pick one, because the Champions League is such a beautiful competition."

Fast-forward to May and the semi-final line-up consisted of Barcelona, Liverpool, Tottenham and Ajax. Surprise results? Or maybe the Argentine megastar isn't as good at punditry as he is dribbling. Either way, he wasn't hiding his desire to win the European Cup and he and Barcelona must have fancied their chances when they reached the last four, understandably so.

Liverpool hadn't won silverware since 2012, Tottenham were trophy-less since 2008 and Ajax's young players were the first to take their club to a Champions League semi-final since 1997. Meanwhile, Barça and Real had won the last five Champions Leagues between them, and Sevilla and Atletico Madrid four of the previous five Europa Leagues.

That's half-a-decade of Spanish dominance on the European scene and with Messi accompanied by ex-Reds Luis Suarez and Philippe Coutinho, plus Ivan Rakitic behind them, they had some serious firepower demonstrated by a statistic showing they had netted in every home game played in the previous 15 months. But they weren't the only ones brimming with confidence.

Sadio all smiles at the Nou Camp pre-match press-conference

Liverpool travelled to the semi-final first leg at the Nou Camp on the back of ten straight wins in the Premier League and Champions League, scoring 28 goals and conceding only seven along the way. The feeling was that Klopp had his team primed to score away-goals, just like they had in Munich and Porto, and the Reds also had the newly-crowned PFA player of the year in their ranks.

"It's pretty difficult to put into words," said Virgil van Dijk after being voted the best footballer in English football by his peers. "I think it's the highest honour you can get as a player, to get voted player of the year by the players you play against every week. It's special. I'm very proud and honoured to receive it."

Inevitably much of the build-up to the first-leg focused on Van Dijk v Messi. Could the big Dutchman stop Barça's all-time great? Or would Messi add to his tally of 24 goals against English clubs at a stadium where he had only ever lost one of 31 knockout matches?

That defeat, incidentally, came against Liverpool in 2007 and the Reds' unbeaten record in four trips to the Nou Camp, and their status as the only English club to beat Barça there (also doing so in 1976), added to the sense of optimism as thousands of LFC fans descended on Catalonia.

Barcelona away. Over 98,000 in the Nou Camp. Is there a more daunting game in European football? Arguably not, but the perception that Barça weren't the team of old, the team that had Xavi, Iniesta and Neymar, coupled with the belief that Liverpudlians had in Jürgen Klopp and his team, fuelled the positive vibes.

Placa Reial, just off La Rambla, was a smoke-filled sea of songs and scarf-twirling with banners like 'LIVERPOOL FC SCOUSE POWER' hung between palm trees and lamp-posts. The Philharmonic Pub, on Calle Mallorca, was taken over by members of the Barcelona branch of the Official Liverpool Supporters Club.

Other fans hung around outside Hotel Sofia, hoping to catch a glimpse of the Liverpool players during their stay there, while some Reds were spotted on old-fashioned versions of Barcelona's trixis – pedal-powered tuk tuks – being toured around the city, beers in hand, singing *Si Señor*.

That Bobby Firmino tribute tune was among those belted out at the pre-match BOSS Night in Barça.

UEFA CHAMPIONS LEAGUE
MADRID 19
FINAL
UEFA CHAMPIONS LEAGUE
OFFICIAL MATCH BALL
adidas

WE COLOR FOOTBALL
FCBARCELONA
20 59
ATION for children

The captain keeps a cool head

An incredible 1,500 Reds packed into Razzmatazz – a nightclub that normally only opens at midnight – for a five-hour singing session from 1pm onwards. How many other sets of supporters have you heard of filling an entire nightclub on a European away-trip before a match? *Ninguna.*

Klopp, of course, was focusing on events on the pitch. "Messi said at the start of the season that they wanted to bring back this cup – that sounded already like a threat to me!" he told the press.

"Now we are here, we want to go to the final as well. There's home advantage for Barcelona and we have the home advantage next Tuesday, then we will see who could use the advantage more."

The Nou Camp may be one of world football's biggest, most iconic stadiums, but the away-end is also one of the worst. Visiting supporters are situated high up in the Gods with a perspex screen, full of scratches, and netting hung from metal poles directly in front of them.

When the sunlight reflects off the perspex, as it does before sunset, it makes the view even worse, although with only sky above you it's not the place to be on a wet night. It isn't the best of places to be when your team are losing, either, as the travelling Kop found out.

Firmino had missed the 5-0 Friday night Premier League win against Huddersfield Town five days earlier with a groin injury and was considered only fit enough to start on the bench in Barça, so Klopp had a decision to make. Would he replace him with Divock Origi or Daniel Sturridge?

He surprised everyone by opting for Gini Wijnaldum, playing him at the tip of a midfield diamond with Naby Keita, James Milner and Fabinho behind. It was a ploy that allowed Liverpool to dominate possession in the first half, something Barça weren't used to in Camp Nou, but the Reds lacked a cutting edge.

Sadio Mane headed an early chance wide and with 20 minutes on the clock Keita went down with a groin problem. He tried to run it off but four minutes later his number was up. Jordan Henderson came on, Keita's season was over.

As the Reds reshuffled Barça took advantage. Jordi Alba guided a low cross into the box and Suarez pounced to slide the ball past Alisson for his first-ever goal against Liverpool.

"In the build up to the game it's nice to talk about how massively grateful I am to Liverpool for all they gave me," he told the *Daily Mail* in the pre-match build-up.

14

0:0
25:31
13

Liverpool see a lot of the ball but it's former hero Luis Suarez who opens the scoring

"But you know me – once I'm on the pitch there will be no friendships, no companions, no thought for all the lovely moments.

"I'll defend the colours of Barcelona with all the pride in the world."

True to his word, after scoring Suarez ran behind the arc-shaped space behind the goal with his arms raised before sliding across the turf on his knees and pointing towards the sky.

For Liverpool fans it hurt, but deep down they understood, too.

Suarez, much like he had been for Liverpool over those three memorable seasons at Anfield (2011-14), was a constant menace in the Catalan colours, tearing around that big, wide pitch, chasing down opponents and contesting every ball before he was replaced three minutes into added-time by fellow forward Ousmane Dembele, more of whom later.

For all that, Mane could have equalised before the break but lifted a shot from Henderson's pass over the Barça bar, while after the half-time interval the Reds continued to dominate but Milner, twice, and Salah were denied by saves from keeper Marc-Andre ter Stegen.

Then Messi took over.

Liverpool were one of the few clubs he'd never previously scored against, but that changed in the

So close for Firmino and Milner as the visitors take the game to Barça

Standard Chartered
LFC

LENGLET
15
unicef
pepsi

MESSI
10
unicef
SERGIO
5
unicef
7

Sometimes you just have to admire a moment of sheer brilliance… Messi's free-kick makes it 3-0

BARCELONA
MESSI 10

The world's best player

75th minute. The ball broke fortunately in the box to Suarez, who improvised by nudging it goalwards with his knee. Clunk. It struck the crossbar but, like a magnet, rebounded straight to Messi who nonchalantly controlled it on his chest and tapped it over the line. Two-nil. The Nou Camp came alive.

Seven minutes later he was at it again, this time curling home a free-kick from over 30 yards out.

Technically-speaking Messi had moved the ball five yards further forward from where the foul on him was initially conceded by Fabinho, but his free-kick – his 600th career goal for Barcelona – was unstoppable, beating a full-stretch Alisson who couldn't quite get a glove on it.

Barça's 'GOAT'– 'greatest of all time' – had left the Reds with a mountain to climb, and set a new Champions League record as Barça extended their unbeaten home run in the competition to 32 games, but this wasn't over.

Some TV companies were still eulogising over the replays when Firmino, on for Wijnaldum, beat Ter Stegen with a low angled-shot only for Rakitic to clear off the goalline. The ball fell to Salah but he thumped it against the post when an away-goal seemed inevitable.

Five minutes of stoppage-time was added on, but still the game continued and in the 97th minute Barça broke clear on the counter-attack from a Liverpool corner. Messi, as Mane chased him down, squared the ball for substitute Dembele, who only had Gerard Pique near him and Alisson to beat.

"IT WOULD HAVE BEEN BETTER GOING TO ANFIELD WITH A FOUR-GOAL ADVANTAGE... THIS IS A TERRIFIC RESULT BUT WE'RE GOING TO A GROUND WHERE THE CROWD WILL GET BEHIND THEM"

Four-nil – at least it should have been. The French striker weakly clipped the ball into the arms of the Reds keeper. And then the final whistle blew.

"It would have been better going to Anfield with a four-goal advantage, but this is a terrific result," said Messi. "We were so close to the fourth goal at the end.

"The 3-0 is a very good result, but it's not definite because we are going to a great stadium where the crowd will really get behind their team."

True. But surely not even Liverpool at Anfield could overturn a 3-0 deficit against the mighty FC Barcelona. Could they?

When Suarez met Robbo

BARCELONA 3
LIVERPOOL 0

Nou Camp - Semi-final first leg
Wednesday 1 May 2019 - Kick-off 8pm
Goals: Suarez (26), Messi (75, 82)

FC BARCELONA (4-3-3):
Ter Stegen, Sergi Roberto (Alena 94), Pique, Lenglet, Jordi Alba, Rakitic, Sergio Busquets, Vidal, Coutinho (Semedo 60), Suarez (Dembele 93), Messi (C).
Subs not used: Arthur, Cillessen, Malcom, Umtiti.
Booked: Lenglet, Alba, Suarez.

LIVERPOOL (4-3-3):
Alisson, Gomez, Matip, Van Dijk, Robertson, Milner (C) (Origi 84), Fabinho, Keita (Henderson 24), Salah, Wijnaldum (Firmino 78), Mane.
Subs not used: Mignolet, Lovren, Shaqiri, Alexander-Arnold. Booked: Fabinho.

Attendance: 98,299. Referee: Bjorn Kuipers.

OFFICIAL LIVERPOOL FC MATCHDAY PROGRAMME
LIVERPOOL FC
UEFA CHAMPIONS LEAGUE
SEMI-FINAL
SECOND LEG
FC BARCELONA

UEFA
CHAMPIONS
LEAGUE
MADRID 19
FINAL
OFFICIAL
MATCH BALL
VERPOOL FC
SEMI-FINAL
FC BARCELONA

YOU'LL NEVER WALK ALONE
LIVERPOOL
FOOTBALL CLUB
EST • 1892
UEFA CHAMPIONS LEAGUE
SEMI-FINAL - 2ND LEG
LIVERPOOL FC v
FC BARCELONA
ANFIELD STADIUM
7 MAY 2019

Suarez: fond memories but in no mood for sentiment

"**When the curtain comes down on this season, and for many years to come, Liverpool fans will bond over the belief and the disbelief of this night. 'The Barcelona game', they'll say, and that'll be all they need to say. A night when Anfield heaved with the heft of the impossible, when a crowd of thousands and an audience of millions lost itself in the mad, dangerous intoxication of football."**

Jonathan Liew, writing in *The Independent*, the morning after the night before. The morning after Tuesday 7 May. The morning after one of the most extraordinary nights of football ever witnessed at Anfield. The morning after a Liverpool win so epic that as you lifted the duvet and blinked in the morning light you dared not pinch yourself, just in case.

Liverpool 4 Barcelona 0.

That's Liverpool four, Barcelona nil, on a night when the Redmen needed to win by four goals to reach the final of the UEFA Champions League. And they did the incredible, the seemingly impossible, without two of their most important, established players.

Three days earlier the travelling Kop had spent Saturday night on the Toon, aka Newcastle, singing about a Belgian to the tune of a 1993 Eurodance hit by an Italian-based Danish singer called Whigfield. As you do, when you're a Liverpool supporter.

"Saturday night and I like the way you move – Divock Origi!" After coming on to score a dramatic 96th-minute winning goal against Everton – his third Merseyside derby strike – in December, he'd already earned himself cult-status on the Kop. But May 2019 would be the month when he wrote his name into Liverpool folklore as a bonafide Reds legend.

With the scoreline at 2-2 in a must-win Premier League game against Newcastle United at St James' Park, striker Mo Salah was forced off with concussion. Origi took his place and four minutes from time he rose highest to head Xherdan Shaqiri's free-kick into the net.

The belief and momentum that winning goal sent coursing through the veins of the Liverpool players should not be underestimated. Klopp called them "mentality monsters" and they took that must-win, will-win attitude into the Barcelona game.

The concussion that Salah suffered at Newcastle prevented him from playing against Barcelona. Whether he felt okay to participate or not, medical rules prevented him from doing so. It was a huge blow, not least because

Bobby Firmino was also sidelined with the groin problem that had meant he was only on the bench at the Nou Camp.

Firmino was the sole player to have appeared in all 39 of Liverpool's European games since Klopp was appointed as manager. Going into a semi-final second leg against Barcelona, when a four-goal victory was required, without him and Salah would be unchartered territory.

"Two of the world's best strikers are unavailable tomorrow," said Klopp in his pre-match press-briefing. "That's not the best idea when you need to score four goals against Barcelona. It doesn't make life easier but we will try to do it.

"We want to celebrate the Champions League campaign. If we can do it, wonderful. If not, then fail in the most beautiful way."

Barcelona coach Ernesto Valverde was questioned about his side's character. A year earlier, in the Champions League quarter-final, they had beaten a Roma team, with Alisson in goal, 4-1 at Camp Nou only to lose the second leg 3-0 in Rome. Could they see the job out this time?

"It's an experience to learn from, but the good thing about football is you always get another chance," he told reporters. "Nothing in football is written, you have to go out there and do it.

"Looking at this full press conference and all the tickets that have been sold, I don't think there is any danger of that [complacency] happening. But Liverpool are a good team, so who knows what could happen?

"We need to ignore the first leg, it would be an error to think that would help us. We're playing at Anfield in front of a very difficult crowd because of the passion and the atmosphere they generate. We've played at big stadiums like San Siro and Old Trafford and done

well this season, I think we can cope with the pressure."

The return of Luis Suarez and Philippe Coutinho to Anfield added extra spice to the occasion and the Uruguayan went on the charm-offensive in the LFC matchday programme. "I am excited to once again feel what it means to play at Anfield," he said, "this time with a different shirt because I defend the Barça colours.

"I am still a Liverpool fan. I like to follow their matches. Their fans are the 12th man because of the way they feed and support the team...you have to play against all of the fans."

Amid a deafening noise his words would fall on deaf ears, but those that Klopp penned in the programme, which featured a Gaudi-inspired design on the front cover, sounded like they could have come from Bill Shankly himself.

"Here is one thing everyone inside Anfield knows, including our opponents. This Liverpool never stops. This Liverpool never quits. This Liverpool gives everything at all times. Whatever happens this Liverpool leaves it all on the pitch and nothing left for regrets. We don't do 'if only'.

"Tonight we ask of our boys to go again. DIg even deeper than they have already. The amazing thing is that they need no words, no encouragement, no outside motivation. They don't seek excuses. They are ready – they want this opportunity. They want to go again and never stop. They have their own answers. This is why they are giants."

When Klopp walked through the Shankly Gates in 2015 he said he wanted to turn Liverpool fans from "doubters into believers." The Barcelona game proved that he had. Never before had the Reds overturned a first-leg three-nil deficit in Europe. To even suggest that duck could be broken against a Barcelona team captained by Messi seemed fanciful.

Ready?

Seven minutes gone, Origi scores
… and Anfield believes even more

Rakuten
27
14
20

Standard
Chartered

L.F.C.
Standard
Chartered
27
23
10

Gini sweeps home no2 and carries the ball back to the centre-spot

Yet the Liverpool supporters who edged through the turnstiles – after the team coach was welcomed on Anfield Road in exuberant style – still believed. They still fancied a comeback.

Perhaps, in the back of some minds, it felt unlikely. Inconceivable, that nobody truly thought they'd be going home that night checking SkyScanner for flights to Madrid. But outwardly the poker faces didn't flinch.

Yes, Liverpool were short-stacked, but Anfield has always been an ace up our sleeves on the big European occasions and Klopp had assembled a team of diamonds with both heart and ability in spades.

If any club could do it, it was Liverpool and one Kop anthem was sung with particular gusto: "Bring on yer Internazionale, bring on yer Roma by the score, Barcelona, Real Madrid…" We all know the rest!

The previous season, en route to the Champions League final in Kiev, Kopites had seen their team score three goals in 31 minutes at home to Manchester City in the quarter-final and put five goals past Roma in 69 semi-final minutes.

Now the target was four plus a clean-sheet, and as scores of flags waved on the Kop and the players walked out to a cacophony of noise before *You'll Never Walk Alone* was sung at full-tilt and the Champions League theme tune was played, you could almost smell the defiance in the air.

Within a minute you could see it on the pitch.

Less than 60 seconds were on the clock when Messi crashed to ground under a challenge from Fabinho, right under referee Cuneyt Cakir's nose. The official saw that Fabinho had got the ball and waved play on.

Messi sat on the turf, his back to the Kop, remonstrating for a split-second until he felt the palms of Andy Robertson's hands momentarily push down on the back of his neck before the left-back strode away.

It was a proper 'welcome to Anfield' moment from the Scotland captain, perhaps not in the same way that Tommy Smith or Graeme Souness would have done in years gone by when referees allowed ball-and-all tackles, but it told Messi that he was in for a battle.

It also showed that the occasionally niggly tactics Barça had deployed at the Nou Camp hadn't been forgotten.

The Kop saw exactly what Robbo had done and they loved it. He'd set the tone and the volume at which they belted out "Oh Andy Andy, Andy, Andy, Andy, Andy Robertson," in response must have shook girders back in his native Glasgow.

Anfield was electric, turbo-charged, with the players plugged into the atmosphere. Not only does such support lift them, it gives opponents the footballing equivalent of the yips.

All of a sudden the seemingly easy becomes unfathomably difficult, as Jordi Alba can testify.

With seven minutes on the clock the Spanish international left-back attempted to cushion a header, from Joel Matip's long ball, to Clement Lenglet. He directed it straight into the path of Sadio Mane instead.

In the blink of an eye Jordan Henderson had raced into the box, after latching onto Mane's pass, and side-footed a shot goalwards with his left peg. Marc-Andre ter Stegen saved, but only pushed the ball into the path of that man Origi, in from the start instead of Firmino. One-nil.

"They've scored!" yelled BT Sport commentator Darren Fletcher. "There's one back! Divock Origi!"

Jordi Alba punched the air in anger. Messi stood with his hands on his hips. Suarez shook his head. Coutinho stared at the ground.

They all knew the last thing, the very last thing, they could do was concede an early goal, to give Liverpool something tangible to fan the flames of optimism.

ORIGI

Two minutes later Wijnaldum's header stuns Barcelona and Anfield erupts

Divock Origi, what have you just done?

Yet there they were, 1-0 down in seven minutes, and with Henderson tucking the ball under his right arm and gesticulating to the Kop with his left as he sprinted back to the half-way line, the ball was back on the centre-spot before Barça knew what had hit them. Game-on.

The Catalans tried to hit back. Alisson tipped a Messi snap-shot over and pushed a weak Coutinho effort away. Messi whipped a first-time effort wide at the Kop end.

Suarez went down under a challenge from Virgil van Dijk and soon came to realise that he wasn't the only one defending his club's colours.

Robertson was then denied by Ter Stegen while Alisson made a vital block from Jordi Alba at the end of a counter-attack, but what proved to be an unlikely game-changing moment occurred five minutes before half-time.

As Robertson and Suarez were running together the Uruguayan seemed to lose his balance slightly and flicked out a leg, catching the Scot just behind him and forcing Robertson to stumble awkwardly.

The pair had reportedly exchanged heated words in the Nou Camp tunnel a week earlier, meaning there was no love lost, but in this clash the Liverpool left-back suffered an injury that forced him off at half-time.

On came substitute Gini Wijnaldum, who later admitted that he was "angry" (in the very best sense) to have been left out of the Liverpool starting XI, with James Milner reverting to emergency left-back.

It proved to be the catalyst for three minutes of madness, of unbridled joy.

It was the 54th minute when Trent Alexander-Arnold conceded possession, with a misdirected header, to Ivan Rakitic. He lifted his arms in frustration, but instead of dwelling on the error immediately chased down Jordi Alba, who had received possession down Barcelona's left, and won the ball back with a tackle that nutmegged the Spaniard.

Alexander-Arnold pushed the ball forward down the right touchline before somehow twisting his body to whip a low, powerful cross that was angled behind him, away from goal. He'd spotted a forward run from Wijnaldum and had the technique to find him.

Wijnaldum met the ball, close to the penalty-spot, ahead of his marker Arturo Vidal and hit a first-time right-footed effort that went through the diving Ter Stegen and into the net. Two-nil.

As Anfield erupted Wijnaldum wrestled the ball out of the arms of the keeper and rushed back to the halfway

Standard
Chartered
LFC
3
Standard
Chartered
LFC

line, turning back towards the Kop with one arm aloft urging still more noise, yet more passion and belief.

Over on the touchline, an exasperated look crossed Valverde's face as he wandered into his technical area with both hands in his trouser pockets. He knew his team were in trouble. And boy were they in trouble.

From the restart, with *Allez Allez Allez* ringing out, the Reds were back on the front-foot and Origi crossed from the right. Too long, but Shaqiri – in for Salah and starting his first Champions League game since the 4-0 win against Red Star Belgrade in October – kept the ball in and clipped it back to Milner.

Instead of standing still, the Swiss midfielder moved towards the touchline, giving Milner the chance to cut inside, creating a two-on-one situation against Vidal.

The Chilean, somewhat rashly, chased Milner down instead of holding his ground before making a half-hearted challenge. His head had gone. Milner easily slipped the ball past him and Shaqiri now had time and space to cross with his wand of a left foot.

He picked out the head of the leaping, unmarked, unchallenged Wijnaldum eight yards from goal. Time stood still, and so did Barça's goalkeeper. Ter Stegen didn't even dive. The ball was in the Kop-end net. Three-nil. Unbelievable!

Pandemonium, bedlam, call it what you like, there were wild celebrations. Just 31 seconds after the game had restarted at 2-0, it was Liverpool 3 Barcelona 0.

"IN THE SECOND HALF THERE WAS ONLY ONE TEAM ON THE PITCH – WHAT WE CANNOT FORGIVE IS THAT WE DID NOT COMPETE AT ANFIELD"

Rakuten

Mo in the T-shirt that became
an overnight sensation

Wijnaldum, who ran in front of the Kop pumping the Liver Bird upon his chest before being mobbed by his team-mates including substitutes Dejan Lovren, Ben Woodburn and Rhian Brewster, had got them both.

"He's been on the pitch for ten minutes!" cried BT Sport co-commentator Steve McManaman before losing his head himself and forgetting the goalscorer's first name. "Gio Wijnaldum! Two in two minutes for him, what a ten minutes, what an impact!"

The travelling Barça fans, who'd contributed to the atmosphere throughout with their own version of *Allez Allez Allez*, were now stood in stunned silence. In the Main Stand, Rangers boss Steven Gerrard, no stranger to Anfield European nights, sat with the palms of his hands clasped together, as if in prayer.

Coutinho was given the hook and trudged off. Vidal followed him soon after. Alisson made a smart save at his near-post to deny Messi after a corner routine caught the Reds out, but they didn't switch off in the way Barcelona did in the 79th minute after Alexander-Arnold forced a corner off Jordi Alba.

Rafa Benitez, Liverpool's 2005 Champions League-winning manager, spoke time and time again about how small details make a difference at the highest level. In Istanbul, for instance, Vladimir Smicer's goal, to make it 3-2, came after AC Milan's Kaka chose to tie his bootlace instead of marking Didi Hamann from a seemingly innocuous throw-in. By the time he tried to chase Hamann down the German had slipped the ball into the path of Smicer, who fired home. Small detail, big goal.

For many years Anfield didn't have ballboys, a quirk that added to the uniqueness of the place, but now young players from the LFC Academy fulfil the role on matchdays. Against Barcelona, unusually for Klopp, Liverpool adopted the multi-ball system. Instead of waiting for the same ball to be retrieved, the youngsters threw another one on to speed the game up.

A 14-year-old ballboy by the name of Oakley Cannonier simply did his job when Alexander-Arnold forced that 79th-minute corner. He immediately threw a different ball to the Liverpool right-back while Origi kicked the other ball off the pitch to him. Small detail, big impact.

Alexander-Arnold placed the ball and shaped to move

Only at Anfield

away from the corner-flag as Shaqiri came over towards him. But suddenly he moved back and whipped a low-trajectory corner in the direction of Origi, who was stood alone, eight yards from goal.

Most of the Barcelona team had their backs to the ball. Some were looking for their man to mark, others were adjusting their sock ties. Ter Stegen was stood almost on the edge of his six-yard box shouting at his defenders and clapping his gloves to cajole them, but he wasn't looking at the ball which, by now, was skimming towards Origi.

The Barcelona goalkeeper and Gerard Pique, who was also on the edge of the six-yard box, suddenly saw the ball out of the corner of their eyes, but it was too late. Origi connected with his instep and lifted the ball into the top-corner. Four-nil.

It was an unusual goal and a surreal moment, but perfectly legitimate and even though the Barça players hoped some kind of offence had been committed there was nothing they could do about it. A lack of concentration and some quick thinking from a 20-year-old Scouser had undone them. They'd crumbled in the maelstrom.

While hugs, kisses, pile-ons and piggy-backs were ongoing in the stands – and it all happened so quickly that many Liverpool supporters inside Anfield didn't see what had occurred until watching replays later that night – Suarez was stood in front of the Kop muttering to himself, gesticulating at his team-mates, hands on hips.

"The days after, back in Barcelona, were the worst moments of my life and career, I wanted to disappear from the world," he admitted in an interview with Fox Sports six weeks later. "Everyone could see I was in a very bad way. I had days I didn't want to do anything, they were very difficult moments.

"I didn't see it [coming] because we are Barcelona and we thought we'd have two or three chances to score. But we became nervous, we gave stupid passes away, we didn't show the right attitude.

"After the game no-one could say anything. There was sadness, bitterness and disappointment because we knew we'd given an awful image."

There were still 11 minutes and stoppage-time to play after Origi's goal, but Barça were shot. When the final whistle went, without them creating anything of note to get the one goal back that would have put them through on away goals, Kop chants of 'We shall not, we shall not be moved' – which teenage substitute Brewster was spotted on the bench singing along to, caught up

NEVER
GIVE
UP
L.F.C.
BETVICTOR
Standard
Chartered

Standard
Chartered
#EQUAL GAME
RESPECT

in the atmosphere – subsided for a loud, guttural roar of delight.

Liverpool had done it. Liverpool were, somehow, in another Champions League final. And as the celebrations began, with Klopp, his players and staff lining up in front of the Kop for a communal singing of *You'll Never Walk Alone*, a beaming Salah ran onto the pitch wearing a t-shirt with the words 'NEVER GIVE UP' emblazoned across the front. It summed up Liverpool – the football club and the city – perfectly.

"I said to the boys before the game it was impossible," a smiling Liverpool manager said afterwards, "but because it's you, I say we have a chance."

Barcelona's players had marched off the pitch as quickly as they could. Fluorescent yellow isn't the colour to be wearing when you've just blown a 3-0 Champions League semi-final lead.

Had their plane home been parked outside you suspect they'd have got on it without taking their boots off.

Messi later admitted he was "still recovering from what happened in Liverpool. In the second half there was only one team on the pitch. That was the biggest mistake, that we did not compete, that we let ourselves down.

"What we cannot forgive is that we did not compete at Anfield."

They knew what was coming on Merseyside. They'd heard the stories. The atmosphere was no secret. They had two high-profile ex-Reds in their team and Messi. But even they, the mighty Barcelona, couldn't deal with an Anfield European night. And this, for many Reds, was Anfield's greatest European night of them all.

"This is Liverpool's gift," wrote Jonathan Liew in *The Independent*. "To rip up what you thought you knew about football and footballers, to take you – mentally and physically – to a place you don't know and never wanted to go. To make your eardrums ring and your sinuses twang and your heart thump to the point where it's all you can think about.

"To the point where you start to question yourself. To the point where you don't realise you've left a massive gap in your left channel until it's just a fraction of a second too late."

Barcelona went back to Barcelona. Liverpool were going to Madrid.

LIVERPOOL 4
BARCELONA 0

Anfield - Semi-final second leg
Tuesday 7 May 2019 - Kick-off 8pm
Goals: Origi (7, 79), Wijnaldum (54, 56)

LIVERPOOL (4-3-3):
Alisson, Alexander-Arnold, Matip, Van Dijk, Robertson (Wijnaldum 46), Henderson (C), Fabinho, Milner, Shaqiri (Sturridge 90), Origi (Gomez 85), Mane. Subs not used: Mignolet, Lovren, Brewster, Woodburn. Booked: Fabinho, Matip.

BARCELONA (4-3-3):
Ter Stegen, Sergi Roberto, Pique, Lenglet, Jordi Alba, Vidal (Arthur 75), Busquets, Rakitic (Malcom 80), Messi, Suarez, Coutinho (Semedo 60). Subs not used: Cillessen, Umtiti, Vermaelen, Alena. Booked: Busquets, Rakitic, Semedo.

Attendance: 55,212. Referee: Cuneyt Cakir.

THE FINAL COUNTDOWN AND A DATE WITH DESTINY…

LFC
6

The Tuesday before the final brings
a bumper press-conference to Melwood

LA SEXTA

Tottenham Hotspur v Liverpool

Red-and-white bunting – *bunting!* Where do you even get it from? Chequered flags, homemade banners, scarves new and old ("your dad wore that in 1977, never been washed"), life-size cardboard cutouts of Mo, Bobby, Sadio and Virgil to frighten the Evertonians, silver-foil European Cups even bigger than the real thing... Come on you mighty, magnificent, mind-blowing Reds!

All over the city of Liverpool, and most probably dotted around the entire country – make that the whole world – in the beautifully mad build-up to the Champions League final, from the moment Jürgen Klopp's men pulled off that miracle in the second leg against Barcelona, whole houses and entire streets were decked out in devotion.

Around the same time a short film appeared on LFCTV as the club's media stoked the pre-match excitement and anticipation with some compelling output.

Seasoned Kopite Stephen Monaghan reflected on Liverpool's eight previous European Cup/Champions League finals, all of which he'd been to, and perfectly caught the mood among the fans.

"Liverpool's my life," he began. "I started on this journey in the mid-Sixties with my dad and he took me everywhere."

'Mono' recalled the glory that was Rome in 1977, then Wembley the following year, Paris in 1981, and Rome once more in 1984. "We were proud to come from Liverpool. We were proud that we were second-to-none in the football world."

He took his own son to Istanbul in 2005. "The team came back from the dead and I'm not ashamed to say I started crying. I had my own son with me then and I told him: 'This is for you, this is for your grandad'.

"This is what football does to you, what Liverpool Football Club does to you. When you get to a final you start thinking of memories, the friends that you've lost who you went to the match with…

"To win the European Cup, it's the ultimate for me."

Joel and Gini do the honours

The current manager and the players could not fail to have felt the pulse of the people, or noticed all those suburban shrines as they drove into Melwood on Tuesday 28 May, another of those sunny-but-breezy-and-bound-to-cloud-over-and-bucket-it-down mornings that characterised the early summer of 2019. Not that they'd ever needed any reminders about just how passionate and proud the red fanbase was.

After the final Premier League game of the season, against Wolves at Anfield, vice-captain James Milner had called the supporters "unbelievable – they've lifted us all year when we've needed them, they've stuck with us when it's been tough in games. The boys deserve a bit of silverware – and the fans do, too."

Now his team-mates Joel Matip and Gini Wijnaldum faced the press on the final media-day back home, a few days after the squad had returned from a week of warm-weather training in Marbella and 72 hours before they flew out to Madrid for the biggest footballing weekend of their lives.

It was Klopp, though, who kicked off proceedings indoors at Melwood, holding the throng of journalists in thrall, oozing charm and charisma, effortlessly switching from English to German, answering good questions and daft with warmth, thoughtfulness, humour and civility.

After the disappointment of Kiev, he recalled, when it'd felt like everything that could go wrong did go wrong against Real Madrid, "the plan was [that] we come again, we will be there again – and now we are. That's just incredible. Pretty much every team that lost the final would think: we'll put that right at some point, but not a chance next year'. And we have the chance."

His team of 2018/19, he declared, "is not even to compare with the team of last year… I was never worried about the future. I am *not* worried about the future. It was always clear that with this team we would have more chances."

All the same, he continued, "the Champions League final is a rare one because obviously a lot of clubs are only built to be there in the final or to win it. We are not. But [the fact] that we are there again is a pure show of the will of the boys. They wanted to be there and they are there and that's brilliant.

"I've never been part of a final with a better team than this. I'm not so surprised because the boys are, how we call it, a 'mix-up' – potential with attitude – in the best way I ever saw or experienced. That's just brilliant, it's exceptional, and that has brought us to where we are."

Klopp's parting shot ahead of the final against familiar opponents from the Premier League? That it would almost certainly be tight but "let's play a difficult game, and let's win it."

Tottenham Hotspur. The Cockerel against the Liver Bird. Who'd have thought it? Spurs had earned their shot at glory from the longest of odds: securing second spot

Last pre-final training session on the lush Melwood grass

Feet firmly on *terra firma* as the squad touch down at Adolfo Suarez Airport

Hello you big inflatable beauty

Session inside the Wanda Metropolitano the night before the big match

behind Barcelona in their group on the final matchday having lost their first two matches and drawn the third, then going on to knock out a formidable-looking Borussia Dortmund, Pep Guardiola's Manchester City – favourites for some – and the new young demi-gods of Ajax.

Respect most definitely due, and the vast majority of Liverpool supporters knew that the North Londoners – even if some of their own followers were protesting otherwise – would prove an exceptionally tough nut to crack.

Mauricio Pochettino's men arrived in Madrid a little before Klopp's, who touched down on Friday lunchtime. Even so, Liverpool's advance-party of fans had already staked out the Spanish capital as their own.

As usual they got there by any means possible, leading one female Liverpudlian wag to tweet: "Men can't plan [bleep] when it comes to women but [bleep] they can plan how to get from Liverpool to [bleep] Madrid without a direct flight for the footie." To be fair, there were practically as many female fans over there too!

Maybe it wouldn't feel quite so 'European', so exotic, playing against a team from the same country. That soon changed once supporters left behind the drab weather back home for the Iberian heat, mid-30s and rising.

Here we were again, young and old, male and female, local and global, all bound by the same ties, posting and liking and retweeting and hugging pals to whom we'd said with half-hearted bravado in Kiev, "See you in Madrid next year." Seriously – *here we were again.*

'MAKING US ALL SKINT SINCE 2015' proclaimed one flag with a big image of Jürgen Klopp. 'NEVER GIVE UP' said the slogan on countless T-shirts. Not a chance. Compared to the Byzantine routes to Ukraine in 2018 this was a walk in the Buen Retiro, serenaded by singsongs on planes, trains, ferries and automobiles. Seventy-five thousand Reds was the modest estimate.

Madrid: the city where *No pasaran* was once coined in defiance – a war-cry since appropriated by one Kopite flag with a picture of clean-sheet king Alisson.

A place where it all happens outdoors, on the streets, in the sunshine, with so much to see and do but so little time when you're swept away on a *marea roja*, a red tide of emotion, adventure and sheer joy.

While fans partied on Friday night – and mixed with their Spurs counterparts in gloriously good humour – Liverpool's 23-man squad trained on the turf at the Estadio Wanda Metropolitano, the venue for the final.

All present and correct: Alexander-Arnold, Alisson,

Heart and *Sol*: Liverpool fans turning the town red

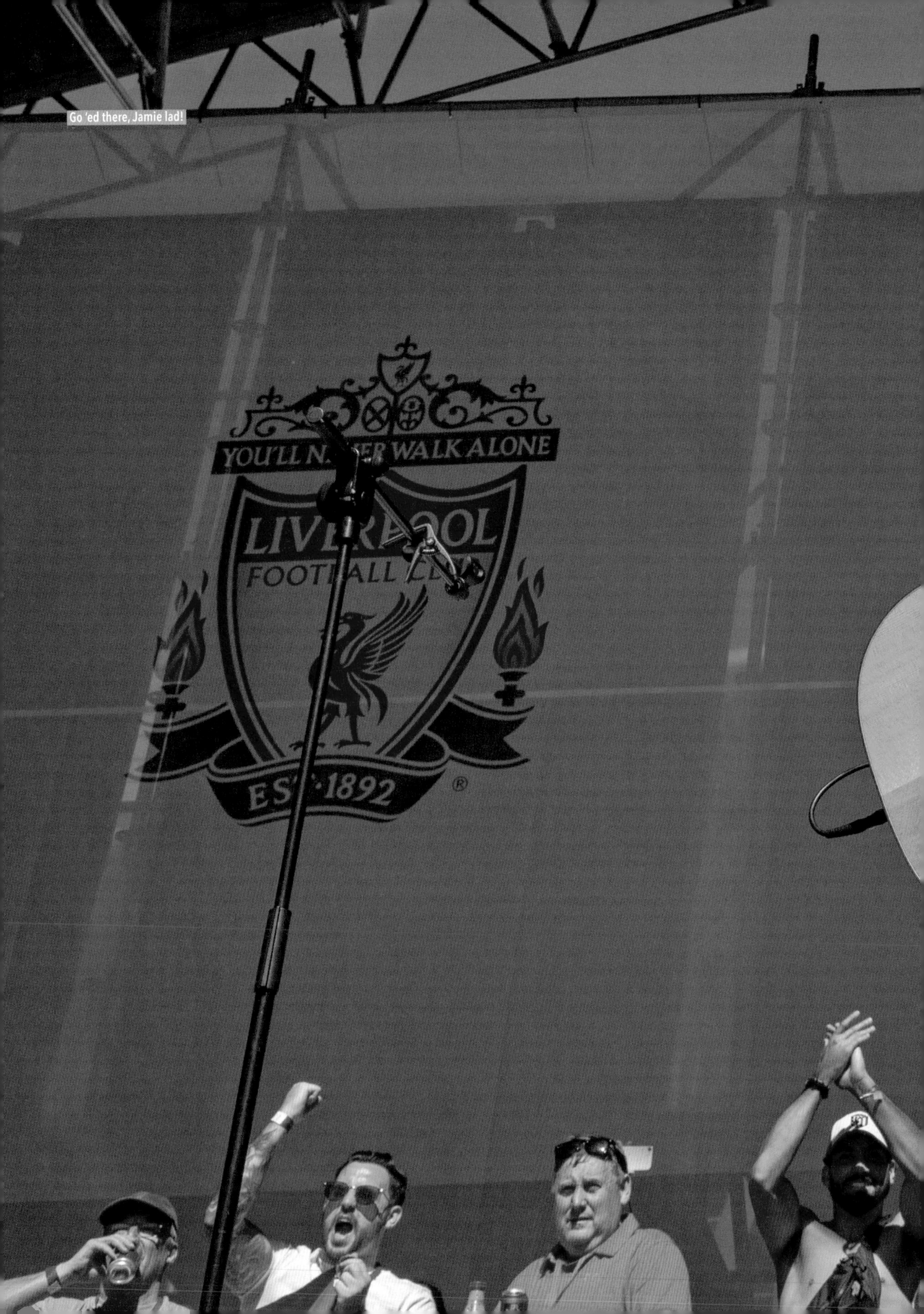

Go 'ed there, Jamie lad!

MADRID
FINAL
rregular Siempre

Brewster, Fabinho, Firmino, Gomez, Henderson, Kelleher, Lallana, Lovren, Mane, Matip, Mignolet, Milner, Moreno, Origi, Oxlade-Chamberlain, Robertson, Salah, Shaqiri, Sturridge, Van Dijk, Wijnaldum. As well as the eleven who'd start the match, a change in UEFA regulations allowed the remaining 12 to be named as substitutes.

The first-choice full-backs did the honours at the accompanying press-conference. Would the hot weather have an impact on the game? Andy Robertson: "It's the same for both teams – we both need to deal with it."

Were Spurs the underdogs? Trent Alexander-Arnold: "In terms of the Champions League and getting to the final, they are – because obviously we got to one last year. But in terms of quality, it's even. They've got world-class players, we've got world-class players. Tomorrow it's a fight till the end to who wants it more."

What about all those Liverpool supporters everywhere in Madrid? Trent: "All the lads are prepared to put everything on the line for the fans, and hopefully everyone who's out here and everyone back home and all around the world will be able to celebrate tomorrow night."

What would it mean to win it for Jürgen? Andy: "We do it for the manager, the coaches and everyone behind the scenes at Melwood. Since he's come here he's changed the way the club is. It would be nice to see him with his hands on the trophy."

Dressed to impress

Allez! Allez! Allez!

Just a Mo...
M.SALAH
11
M.SALAH
11
M.SALAH
11

YNWA
Standard
Chartered

The bit when you just want it to get started

A glimpse into the Liverpool dressing-room

LIVERPOOL
F.C.
WOODPECKER
KIRKBY
WHAT CAN I SAY?
SAY I'M
A DREAMER
NATURAL
ENTHUSIASM
YOU'RE NOTHING
WITHOUT IT
SHANKLY
THE ARKLES DUGOUT
SALAH
AND
COULD HE
PLAY!
OH CAMPIONE
THE ONE AND ONLY
WE'RE LIVERPOOL
BIG BOY
FOOTBALL
FORZA
LIVERPOOL
77 78 81
84 05
LFCFANNEWS
MAURITIUS
LFC Global Family
JFT96
AT THE END OF THE STORM
HUYTON REDS
CONNOISSEURS OF EUROPEAN LAGER
UP THE REDS

The originals, and still the best

We. Are. Here

Red is the colour

Salah prepares to take the spot-kick in front of 63,000 in the ground and a global TV audience of 400 million

AIA
Standard
Chartered
11

He shoots, he scores, he's chased by Hendo… but the boss keeps his cool

Saturday morning, mercury rising. The heat hit you like a sledgehammer as you emerged from the maw of metro station Goya into Plaza Felipe II, the designated LFC fan-park.

Forty-eight years earlier Bill Shankly had stood on the steps of St George's Hall in Liverpool when his team returned beaten but unbowed from the FA Cup final, and declared: "Chairman Mao has never seen a greater show of red strength."

This, around 900 miles from home, was right up there, with thousands of Reds fans still pouring into Madrid.

The club had collaborated with the team behind Liverpool's legendary BOSS Nights to put on the show to end all shows: Cast frontman John Power's stirring version of *You'll Never Walk Alone*; John Barnes in hip-hop heaven and women's footballer and singer-songwriter Chelcee Grimes doing Dua Lipa's *One Kiss*; The Anfield Wrap team on stage as terrace troubadours Kieran Molyneux and Jamie Webster got the bounce going (with retweets by Virgil van Dijk); and DJ and Reds fan Colin Murray smashing it with a left-field set including *Bohemian Rhapsody* and *All You Need Is Love* (Madrid, like everywhere else, idolises the Beatles).

Many in the vast audience didn't have tickets for the final and would be watching in bars and restaurants around the city instead. If nothing could beat being inside the stadium, half-a-dozen more metro stops along line 7, there was some consolation in just being there in Madrid in the middle of it all.

By the time proceedings drew to a close in the fan-

park, the Liverpool end at the Wanda Metropolitano was filling up. If some familiar big flags made it feel like home – the Liver Bird in trainers, Ol' Big Ears with five stars on it, the dancing Kopite from the old *Football Echo*, Anne Williams always remembered – that was the whole idea.

Tony Barrett, the club's head of supporter liaison, would later tweet: "One of the reasons why the Liverpool end looked so spectacular was @SpionKop1906 decided to bring the Kop to Madrid. The effort that they put in to

Trent: terrific

Alisson: just outstanding

Virgil: very good

Origi on for Firmino while Milner replaces Wijnaldum

ORIGI
32
VERTONGHEN
5

Oh Divock...

Yiiirrrrsssssee!!!!!

make this happen was well above the call of duty."

Not present in the ground but surely there in spirit was the daddy of them all: the giant Joey Jones banner from 1977, back when it all began. One of its creators, supporter Phil Downey, would pass away a week later. Thank you, Phil, and god bless.

Ear-drums suitably oscillating as pre-match fireworks went off and Imagine Dragons blasted through their short set, out came the teams and in kicked the nerves – and less than 30 seconds into the action the Reds had a penalty.

Harsh, perhaps, but the ball from Sadio Mane did strike Moussa Sissoko on the shoulder then his hand. Mo Salah went for power, sprinting up and smashing the spot-kick past Hugo Lloris, who'd reacted a little too early, to leave the Spurs fans behind the goal stunned and the other end of the ground in raptures.

Can you score too early? Did nerves kick in? Was the heat a factor? Had three weeks between the end of the domestic season and this fixture caused too much drag?

Definitely, maybe. All a bit of a blur, with sudden shifts in focus.

Trent fired one low but wide of the target. Tottenham got on the ball more and their fans found their voices.

A streaker briefly gatecrashed proceedings. Andy Robbo powered into the Spurs half and saw his fierce drive tipped over the crossbar.

Jordan Henderson ran and passed and tackled with Fabinho and Wijnaldum ably assisting, but no one was taking the game by the scruff of the neck. Upfront for the opposition Harry Kane looked forgivably off-the-pace. Christian Eriksen blazed high on the stroke of half-time.

A breather, as the sun finally set behind the western curve of the stadium, for the 63,000-plus inside and the millions more watching all over the world at different times of the day. Was it a pen, asked Gary Lineker in the BT Sport studio. "No way," said Spurs legend Glenn Hoddle. "Definitely," countered former Reds striker Michael Owen. "You can't put your hand in that position."

No changes for either side as they re-emerged for the second period. Mo and Dele Alli had shots blocked. Jan Vertonghen headed over. Either side of the hour-mark Divock Origi came on for Bobby Firmino and James Milner replaced Gini Wijnaldum.

The Spurs fans sang their anthems. The red end of the stadium, tense for long periods, responded by roaring their heroes forward.

On 69 minutes the magnificent Sadio Mane rode the challenge of Dele Alli and powered cross-field, checking to cut inside Eriksen, apply the burners again and play

UEFA

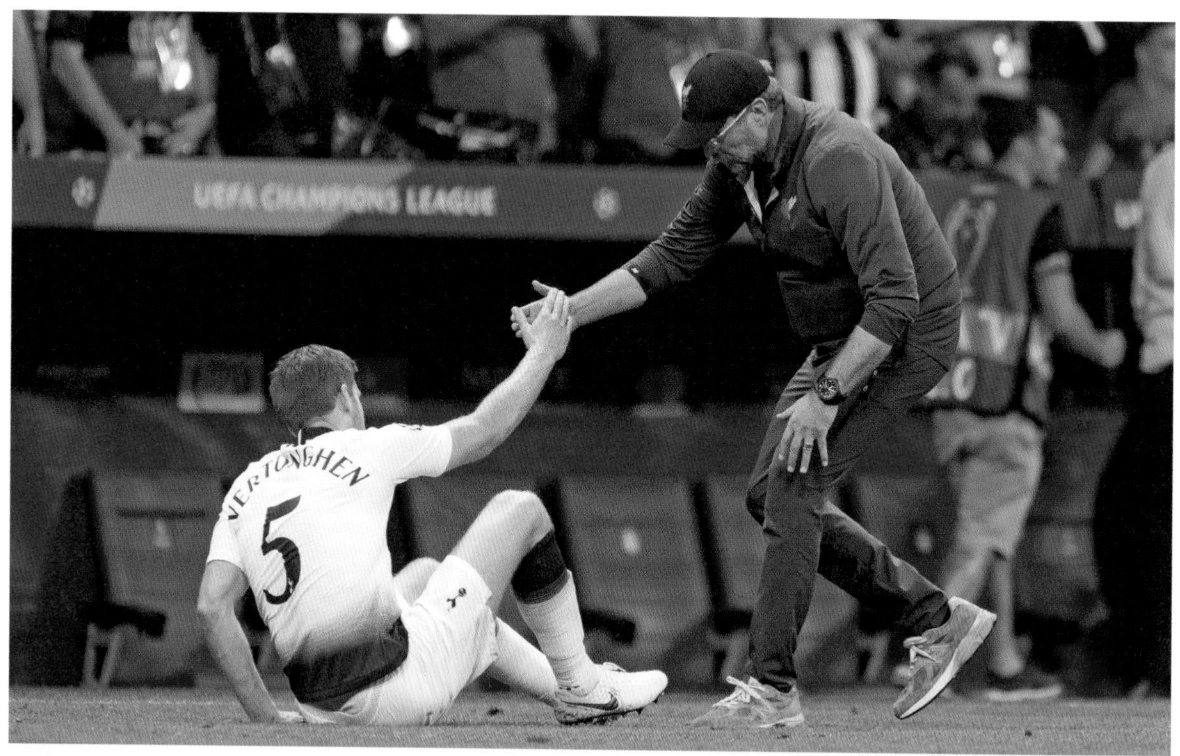

Klopp shows his class while his team race towards the fans in sheer elation

Standard

L.F.C.

UEFA
CHAMPIONS
LEAGUE
RESPECT

the ball into Salah inside the box. Instinctively Liverpool's no11 laid the ball back to Milner whose left-foot shot left Lloris stranded but flashed just past the post. So, so close.

The clock ticked past 10.30pm local time. Darkness had slowly fallen across a moonless sky but Liverpool could see light at the end of the tunnel. Tottenham had to go for it and they did for 15 minutes.

Dele Alli's chip looked deceptively dangerous but Alisson made the catch. Heung-Min Son burst into the box only for Van Dijk, UEFA's man-of-the-match and colossally cool as ever, to intercept. Alisson made a double-save from Son, the main Spurs threat, and substitute Lucas Moura, before getting both gloves on an Eriksen free-kick from the edge of the area to palm it away.

There's a Kopite flag which surfaces on social-media now and again featuring a Liver Bird and just two words: 'ME NERVES'. You either get it or you don't.

There were three minutes of normal time left when Andy Robertson made a typical foray into enemy territory but slightly over-hit his cross. Tottenham left-back Danny Rose, with Mo on his shoulder, wasn't taking any chances, chesting the ball out for a corner from the right. Over jogged James Milner.

All eyes on the number seven. His outswinging delivery just skimmed over the heads of three Spurs players and bounced once before Van Dijk shanked a half-volley, just as he'd done in the build-up to other important goals twice before this season.

The ball ricocheted off substitute Eric Dier who then headed it up into the air in the area. Virgil and Jan Vertonghen leapt together, shoulder to shoulder, and the ball sprang off them and dropped suddenly to Joel Matip who intuitively diverted it wide to the orange-booted Origi in a square-yard of space.

Everyone's favourite Belgian, off the bench and struggling till then to find his touch and feel the game's rhythm, could have been caught flat-footed, could've taken a split-second too long to control the ball, fired it straight into the shins of Toby Alderweireld.

Instead Origi was alert and on his toes, muscle-memory

from a million drills at Melwood teasing the ball out of his feet and opening up his body to shoot hard and low, back across Lloris into the far corner of the net. Oops – Divock broke the internet again.

And with such simplicity, to coin a phrase, the European Cup was won.

At the edge of the box Van Dijk sank face-forward to the floor in joyous relief. Alexander-Arnold ran to the Spurs goal, scooped up the ball and punted it high into the rolling, writhing, tearful mass of red – in the midst of it, down at the front, Stephen Monaghan, the Kopite who'd worn his blood-red heart on his sleeve in that poignant LFCTV documentary, and now there with his lad, going mad, and picked out by one of the cameras behind the goal. You'll have seen it many times by now.

Seven Nation Army by the White Stripes blared out of the PA and just like that became "Ohhh Divock Origi!" Then "We shall not, we shall not be moved!"

Still time for Alisson to save from Son, then Kane, to a mighty cheer from the Liverpool fans, before the final whistle.

Scenes inside the stadium, scenes in bars all over Madrid, scenes back home in the M&S Bank Arena, the Bierkeller, the Shankly Hotel, the Sandon, pubs all over Merseyside, homes everywhere.

Scenes in heaven, if you believe in these things, because this sixth European Cup was as much for loved ones and absent friends as the record books.

The best Champions League trophy-lift ever, followed by some seriously impressive individual efforts!

LIVERPOOL FC
VIRGIL
SALAH
PHOTO

LIVERPOOL FC
LIVERPOOL
eineken

LALLAN

The bumps for the boss and a moment and one for the backroom staff's photo album

It was also for all the young dudes: Liverpool's new legion of bright, savvy boy-and-girl supporters who'd sensed, ever since the Jürgen Klopp juggernaut began to gather pace, that this was their time. We'd conquered all of Europe, again, we were never gonna stop, and we loved this team to bits.

They were made-up for Jordan Henderson, whose sensational captain's trophy-lift raised the bar and then some; who sought out his father at the end of the match for a moving embrace, and who had always put others first.

"I'm so proud to be a part of this football club," he said pitchside. "I've had tough times but I've kept going – just as this club has. It's the best moment of my life, what I dreamed of since I was a kid.

"It's not about me, it's not about me being captain or lifting the trophy, it's about this club, these players, this manager. Now we must keep going and kick on."

Made-up for James Milner, the model pro who'd never taken himself too seriously but was as dedicated and indispensable as they come.

Made-up for Mo after what happened the previous year. Made-up for Mane who'd led the line magnificently all season. Made-up for Bobby Firmino for that big smile and those round-by-round moments of magic.

Made-up for Divock who just wanted to "shine his light" whenever and wherever he could for the team.

Made-up for Gini, one of football's nice guys but a ferocious force of nature against Barcelona. Made-up for Fabinho – his class was never in doubt.

Made-up for Matip, unsung and unfazed and always there. Made-up for Virgil, the big man – what more can you say?

Made-up for Trent, at 20 years 237 days the first player aged under 21 to start in consecutive Champions League finals. "I'm just a normal lad from Liverpool whose dream has just come true."

Made-up for Andy Robbo who'd tweeted back in 2012 as an 18-year-old: "Life at this age is rubbish with no money #needajob."

Made-up for Alisson, who'd settled in so smoothly, on and off the field, jammed with Jamie Webster earlier in the season, FaceTimed his wife and daughter after the final whistle, and without whose late save against Napoli at Anfield in the group-stage finale none of this would have been possible.

Made-up for the Ox and Shaq and Naby and Dejan and Studge, for Simon Mignolet, Joe Gomez, Alberto Moreno, Adam Lallana, Rhian Brewster and Caoimhin Kelleher.

And made-up, of course, for the gaffer, who'd ended his own run of half-a-dozen cup-final defeats and could now talk about six, baby!

On the day of his appointment as manager, on 9 October 2015, he'd said to the press corps at Anfield: "If I am sitting here in four years, I think we will have won one title in this time."

Now, to the world from the Wanda Metropolitano, he said he felt "mostly relief – relief for my family. The last six times we flew on holiday with only a silver medal, it didn't feel too cool.

"We were all crying on the pitch because it means so much to us. It wasn't important for me to touch the cup – I loved seeing the boys having it and seeing some faces in the crowd.

"Going to Liverpool tomorrow with something to celebrate is big and I'm really looking forward to that."

Thousands of Liverpool fans, who knew they wouldn't be back in time, partied in Madrid where, Ernest Hemingway once wrote, "Nobody goes to bed until they have killed the night." It's fair to say that the travelling Kop merrily obliged.

At home that same night euphoric young Reds supporters scaled Anfield's Paisley Gates in celebration

MADRID 19
FINAL
BREWSTER
24

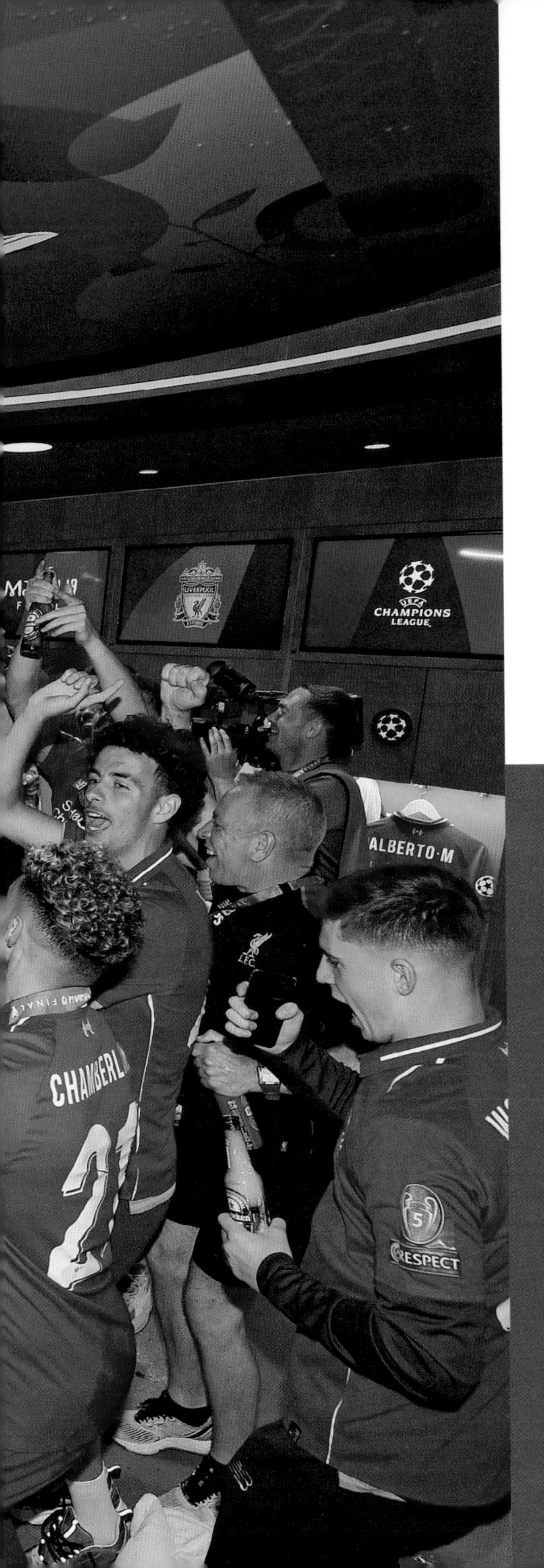

while town pretty much came to a standstill.

Footage emerged on social-media of Central Station thronged with happy fans who'd missed their last trains, singing and dancing and in one instance using a traffic cone as a megaphone!

In their midst, a bronze statue of a Liver Bird unveiled in 2014 in tribute to Reds fan Paul Rice, one of the founders of the Spirit of Shankly supporters union. Paul had died two years earlier at the age of 54 following a battle with leukaemia. He, too, would have been made-up.

A word for Tottenham Hotspur Mauricio Pochettino, so gracious in defeat: "We're all very disappointed [but] I want to congratulate Liverpool, Klopp, the players and the fans because they've had an amazing season."

And for the Spurs supporters in Madrid who were top-class and, in turn, posted only good things online about the red hordes they met on their travels.

Time, just about, to go home. "I might not be a Liverpool FC fan," tweeted one adopted Scouser, "but the city's tendency to go completely mad is a big reason I've called it home for 23 years. Don't go changing..."

As if we would.

TOTTENHAM HOTSPUR 0
LIVERPOOL 2

Estadio Metropolitano, Madrid - Final
Saturday 1 June 2019 - Kick-off 8pm
Goals: Salah (2 pen), Origi (87)

TOTTENHAM HOTSPUR (4-2-3-1):
Lloris (C); Trippier, Alderweireld, Vertonghen, Rose; Sissoko (Dier 74), Winks (Moura 66); Alli (Llorente 82), Eriksen, Son; Kane. Subs not used: Vorm, Gazzaniga, Sanchez, Walker-Peters, Aurier, Foyth, Davies, Wanyama, Lamela.

LIVERPOOL (4-3-3):
Alisson; Alexander-Arnold, Matip, Van Dijk, Robertson; Wijnaldum (Milner 62), Henderson (C), Fabinho; Salah, Firmino (Origi 58), Mane (Gomez 90). Subs not used: Mignolet, Kelleher, Moreno, Lovren, Oxlade-Chamberlain, Shaqiri, Lallana, Sturridge, Brewster.

Attendance: 63.272. Referee: Damir Skomina.

"I'M SO PROUD TO BE A PART OF THIS FOOTBALL CLUB. IT'S THE BEST MOMENT OF MY LIFE, WHAT I DREAMED OF AS A KID. NOW WE MUST KEEP GOING AND KICK ON"

"Look what we've got"

"I wish I'd brought that cushion..."

So to the Sunday morning after the night before – for those who got any sleep – and the start of another unforgettable day of celebration as the city of Liverpool welcomed the European champions home in staggering numbers.

First, though, breakfast! Ahead of their mid-morning flight the squad sat down for some refreshments in their hotel – appropriately named Hotel Eurostars – with James Milner and Adam Lallana having the trophy for company as their table's centrepiece.

It was orange juice rather than a Ribena for the vice-captain on this occasion, however!

Then it was off to the Adolfo Suarez Airport for the two-and-a-half-hour flight back to Liverpool, the cup being passed around the plane by players, staff and officials. Mo Salah even enjoyed a cheeky power-nap clutching the trophy!

Meanwhile, those supporters who had booked day-trips to Madrid on chartered flights had already returned to John Lennon Airport ahead of the first team; a lucky few hundred able to take in the scenes at the Plaza Felipe II fan-park, the Wanda Metropolitano showpiece as well as the celebrations back home to come – quite a 24 hours following Liverpool FC.

The squad touched down on the Speke tarmac at around 1pm to a ceremonial welcome with water-jets forming an arch over the plane. Manager and captain emerged first – along with some additional luggage – followed by the rest of the party for a photo on the stairs, each with gold medals around their necks, before hopping on a coach to Melwood for a swift change ahead of the parade's start at 4pm.

Each player had the new 2019/20 home shirt to wear – complete with 6-times sleeve-patches and a 'Champions of Europe' and '19' name-and-number combo on the back in gold lettering, with several of them wearing their shirts back-to-front to show it off.

Another short coach-journey took them to Allerton Maze (just east of Sefton Park) and the start of the ten-mile route that would take them to the Strand/Dock

From the South End to the Strand an estimated three-quarters-of-a-million welcomed home their heroes

Road via Queens Drive, Mill Bank, West Derby Road, Islington and Leeds Street.

An open-top all-red bus emblazoned with a European Cup graphic and the words 'CHAMPIONS OF EUROPE' was their ride for the next four hours or so. Complete with police escort, two additional buses for club staff, players' families and the media, and a vehicle packed with loudspeakers and confetti launchers, the convoy was good-to-go and on schedule.

The earlier overcast and sprinkly conditions made way for glorious sunshine, too, not that anyone would have missed this regardless – Reds supporters packed the streets from start to finish.

Flags, twirling scarves and red 'pyros' held by supporters wearing jerseys from all LFC eras made a magnificent backdrop as the parade slowly cruised past the fervent crowds.

Children sat on the shoulders of their parents – one of the safer raised vantage-points – while many fans chased alongside the bus to catch the eye of their favourite player or another glimpse of the cup. And it seemed there were even more houses decked out in red-and-white.

Allez Allez Allez, *Ring of Fire*, *Fields of Anfield Road* and songs for Bobby Firmino and Virgil van Dijk were all belted out by fans and players alike.

Some spectators had been here before, a few right back to the days of Bill Shankly, but for many lining the route it was the first time they'd seen not only the trophy but manager Jürgen Klopp and his players 'in the flesh'.

The turnout was estimated at three-quarters-of-a-million – all the more impressive considering so many were still be making their journeys home from Madrid.

Well over 10,000 fans would queue for a photo with the cup at Anfield's Kop Bar a week later, the buzz still in the L4 air.

A special homecoming programme also aired on LFCTV with outside broadcasts from Queens Drive and the Atlantic Tower Hotel's waterfront terrace in the city-centre. Former players John Aldridge, Jason McAteer and Chris Kirkland were there to describe the scenes while videos were posted on social-media from every conceivable angle: street-level to rooftops and just about anything that could be scaled. It was not a day for health- and safety-enthusiasts!

Vice-captain Milner got the driver to stop outside the home of Hillsborough survivor Andrew Devine, confined to a wheelchair following the disaster, ensuring he got a good look at the Champions League trophy.

Goalie Alisson dangled off the back of the bus as he sang along to chants from the crowd. Gini Wijnaldum actually dropped his phone and, with his Instagram live-video still recording, one fan threw it back. Gini, by now in hysterics with fellow Virgil van Dijk, waved down and shouted, "It's still working!"

Stena Line
MUSEUM OF LIVERPOOL
ALBERT DOCK

CHAMPIONS OF EUROPE
WE ARE LIVERPOOL
Q PARK

CHAMPIONS
OF EUROPE
WE ARE LIVERPOOL
THIS MEANS MORE

Later he took time-out from the singalong to sum up the occasion with LFCTV: "It's difficult to put into words – it's something you have to feel, it's phenomenal.

"You see how many people come to see the bus-tour, it's more than I expected. To see grandmas, grandpas, babies, all kinds of ages – you see how much it means to the city."

Goal hero Divock Origi concurred: "Liverpool is celebrating today, we can feel it. It means a lot to the people – I can see it in their eyes and in their reaction."

Van Dijk – when not trying his hand at some impromptu presenting and interviewing for LFCTV on the upper deck of the players' bus – was equally taken-aback by the scale of the reception: "It's something special, you have to really experience it.

"It's unbelievable what it does to the city and obviously to the club as well. I think there's still more to come but it's already been past my expectations."

Some praise from the man who'd set such high standards in his first 18 months at the club.

He continued: "I'm very proud to be sitting on this coach and hopefully we can have more days like this. I'm just taking everything in and enjoying every bit of it with all of these fans."

The interview was even sealed with a kiss from Alisson, kitted out in a Champions of Europe scarf, sunglasses and improvised headscarf. He added: "When you are here feeling the emotion of these people, our supporters, it's amazing.

"I put my heart on the pitch and I gave my best for my team-mates to win the title and bring the cup to Liverpool. This team deserved to win something big this season because we made a great season in the Premier League and the Champions League."

And a word from central defender Dejan Lovren, part of the squad for each of the three European finals under Klopp and finally a winner: "What we did in previous years, unfortunately we lost a couple of finals, but all these people never stopped believing in us. It's a gift to them and they say thank-you.

"Sometimes you need to be knocked down to get up again. It's about character, it's about emotions, it's about many things. I think this team has everything."

The boss meanwhile was in his element. Having fulfilled that promise to bring a major trophy to Anfield within four years of his appointment, he sang along with the crowds and was filmed playfully counting to six on his fingers.

What did he make of the day so far? "I cannot really

RIVER
FESTIVAL
LIVERPOOL
authorised
vehicles
taxi
FINAL
CHAMPIONS
OF EUROPE
YOU'LL NEVER WALK A
LIVERPOO
FOOTBALL CL
EST-1892
NS FINAL

describe it because I cried a little bit as well because it's so overwhelming what the people are doing.

"When you have a direct-eye contact and you see how much it means to them that's touching, it's so intense. Today – wow! It's crazy."

His assistant-manager Peter Krawietz, normally a man of few words, added: "Going to the final again and winning it is unbelievable. It's a fantastic team and we will try to keep this up and go again – we know that we are strong.

"There are not a lot of clubs in the world where you can make this: winning titles and having so much togetherness with the team and the fans."

By this point the parade had reached the waterfront with the skipper holding the cup at the front of the bus. It'd taken over three hours, but the celebrations from here went to another level.

At a little past 7pm, and with the convoy's speaker-system playing *You'll Never Walk Alone* as it passed the Royal Liver Building, fireworks were set off from one of the landmark's famous towers as red confetti filled the air. Jürgen Klopp duly made his way to the front of the bus and raised the cup aloft.

A new generation of fans now had their own homecoming parade to cherish.

Those who were there would never forget.

"EVERYONE IS A BETTER PLAYER
THAN THEY WERE BEFORE..."

L.F.C.

Sometimes it takes an event such as a Champions League triumph to fully comprehend the size of Liverpool FC's fanbase. As if the scenes at the homecoming in the city of Liverpool weren't breathtaking enough, the club's official TV channel LFCTV compiled a film of Reds supporters celebrating all over the world: from Boston to Baghdad, Mumbai to Mexico City, Cairo to Copenhagen, Sapporo to San Jose.

This sixth triumph – and 42nd major trophy overall – put daylight between the Reds and two other continental heavyweights, Bayern Munich and Barcelona, both on five wins. Only Real Madrid with 13, and AC Milan with seven, had won it more times. The Champions Wall at Melwood was duly updated with the number 6 replacing 5 underneath the unmistakable outline of Ol' Big Ears.

Jürgen Klopp's first piece of Reds silverware made him the fourth Liverpool manager to win the trophy after Bob Paisley (1977, 1978 and 1981), Joe Fagan (1984) and Rafael Benitez (2005). All of those names are beloved but arguably not since Bill Shankly has a Liverpool manager enjoyed such a passionate rapport with the fans nor forged such a formidable feeling of unity between players, supporters and football club.

All have felt invested in Klopp's methods from day one with his philosophy of attacking football an onfield reflection of his natural enthusiasm and charisma. Players want to play for him, fans believe fully in him.

After the final whistle in Madrid captain Jordan

L.F.C.
RESPECT

Henderson said, simply: "Without this manager, this is impossible...what he has done is unbelievable."

Virgil van Dijk spoke of "a fantastic future coming up. We have players who want to develop and give everything for the team" while "everyone," added his team-mate Gini Wijnaldum, "is a better player than they were before."

Klopp had been appointed manager three-and-a-half years after Liverpool FC's last trophy, the 2012 League Cup, and just under 18 months after the Reds had come within a whisker of winning the Premier League.

That debut season yielded two finals but defeat to Manchester City in the League Cup then Sevilla in the Europa League. In 2017/18 the Reds returned to the Champions League for the first time in three seasons and confounded expectations by reaching the final in Kiev.

As Klopp would point out in the press-conference before the 2019 final, that loss to Real Madrid "had a big influence on us. I remember we were standing in the queue at the airport on the way home, all in tracksuits, heads down, really disappointed. There were a lot of different emotions [but] it was not allowed to be angry. The plan was that we come again. It was the kick-start for the development of this team, 100 per cent."

Season 2018/19 saw a change. The full-throttle football of previous campaigns gave way to a more pragmatic approach, with defensive reinforcements such as goalkeeper Alisson Becker, centre-back Virgil van Dijk and holding midfielder Fabinho enjoying their first full seasons with the Reds.

Klopp's side were no less exhilarating to watch – indeed Naby Keita had been signed partly for that purpose – but Liverpool also had the best defensive record in the 2018/19 Premier League, conceding just 22 goals – the platform for both a serious title push and a second assault on the Champions League.

Big teams like Bayern Munich and FC Porto were blitzed on their own grounds while Barcelona were blown away at Anfield. Earlier it had taken solidity as well as style to overcome Napoli in the all-important last group game, while the final itself against Tottenham was an exercise in strength, organisation and attitude.

As he enjoyed the post-match celebrations Klopp removed his cap and took a bow before the massed Reds fans. "We sometimes carry the burden of history," he admitted afterwards. No more. His humility is such that he gave all the credit to his players, but this is a Liverpool team very much in his image and Jürgen Klopp's legacy at Anfield is now assured forever.

5
RESPEC

SCROLL OF HONOUR

THE MANAGER, STAFF & PLAYERS

JÜRGEN **KLOPP**
PETER **KRAWIETZ**
PEPIJN **LIJNDERS**
JOHN **ACHTERBERG**
JACK **ROBINSON**
ANDREAS **KORNMAYER**
ANDREW **MASSEY**
PHILIPP **JACOBSEN**
CONALL **MURTAGH**
PAUL **SMALL**
LEE **RADCLIFFE**
GRAHAM **CARTER**
DAVID **RYDINGS**
MONA **NEMMER**
MARK **LEYLAND**
GREG **MATHIESON**
JAMES **FRENCH**
SCOTT **McAULEY**
CHRISTOPHER **ROHRBECK**
RICHIE **PARTRIDGE**
JOE **LEWIS**

FABINHO
VIRGIL **VAN DIJK**
GEORGINIO **WIJNALDUM**
DEJAN **LOVREN**
JAMES **MILNER**
NABY **KEITA**
ROBERTO **FIRMINO**
SADIO **MANE**
MOHAMED **SALAH**
JOE **GOMEZ**
ALISSON **BECKER**
JORDAN **HENDERSON**
DANIEL **STURRIDGE**
ALBERTO **MORENO**
ADAM **LALLANA**
ALEX **OXLADE-CHAMBERLAIN**
SIMON **MIGNOLET**
XHERDAN **SHAQIRI**
RHIAN **BREWSTER**
ANDY **ROBERTSON**
DIVOCK **ORIGI**
JOEL **MATIP**
NATHANIEL **PHILLIPS**
CURTIS **JONES**
GEORGE **JOHNSTON**
KI-JANA **HOEVER**
ISAAC **CHRISTIE-DAVIES**
BEN **WOODBURN**
CAOIMHIN **KELLEHER**
CONOR **MASTERSON**
RAFAEL **CAMACHO**
TRENT **ALEXANDER-ARNOLD**

KOPBOYRED 50
John Paul Abrahams
Andreas Achilleos
David Achilles
Maimarie and Darryl Adair
Brian Adelgaard
Daniel Aebischer
Kevin Douglas Aherne
Kaybird Akinyemi
Nasser Al-Ghanim
John Aldridge
Greg Allen
Wes Allen
Bader Al Qabandi
Lynn Anderson
John Angelovski
Neuza Aniceto
Mona Anjoom-Zaman
Christopher Ann
Ray Annal
Wayne Appleton
Ian Armitage
Kevin Armstrong
Ken Ashun
Lauren Ashun
Lee Ashun
Harri Aston
David Atherton
George Ayscough
Edward Azevedo
Nikhil Azmi
Sam and Daniel Baines
Daniel Baker
Kyle Baker
Vin Fei Ban
Kesha Bangay
Itay Bar Oz
Paul Barber
Frank Barker
Alison Barkley
Anthony Gerard Barkley
Elliot James Barkley
Sophia Autumn Barkley
Mark Barnard
Stuart Barnes
David Barrett
John Paul Barrett
Tony Barry
Jason Bartlett
Samuel Bartlett
Ann-Marie Barton
Adam Bassett
Alex Bayley
Buff Bayley
Myles Bayley
James Beaney
Felix Beard
Rob Beckett
David Bedford
Silvia Behrmann
Bernadette Bennett
Harrison Bennett
John Bennett
John Bennett (Beno)
Michael John Bentley
Suvith Bhothikhun
Joanne Bignall
Tom Billings
Susan Birch
Andy Birchall
Keenan Black-Araujo
Niall Blaney
Matthew Bleasdale
Manjeet Boall
Charlotte Boileau Hayes
Au Yong Boon Eng (Marcus)
Noah Bostock
Dexter Bowring
Jasveer Brach
Brandon-Paul Bradley
Brody-Francis Bradley
David Bradley
Jason Bradley
Arthur Brand
Michael Sean Brett
Patrick Brickley
Rob Bridge
Darren Robert Brockbank
Chris Brooks
Holly Brooks
Steve Brooks
Simon Brotherton
Christine Brown
Claire Brown
James Brown
Jennifer Brown

"What motivates these boys to fight and battle? It is to win for the supporters." Jürgen Klopp appreciates the part Liverpool FC supporters have to play and that's why those of you who pre-ordered Ch6mpions of Europe take your place alongside the manager, staff and players who made the glory of Madrid 2019 possible...

Lee Brown
Liam Brown
Lucas Brown
Michael Shoney Brown
Antonia Bruna Justo
Charlie Bryans Moreland
Dean Buckley
Simon Burgess
Craig Burnett
John Burns
Chad Burns
Evie Burns
Ivy Burns
Joanne Burns
Lacey Burns
Lewis Burns
Lydia Burns
Maisie Burns
Michael Burns
Terry Byrne
Terry Bywater
Joe Cahill
Nick Cahill
Dominic Cain
William Caldwell Whittingham
William Callaghan
Matthew Callon
Michael Cameron
Alan Campbell
David Cardwell
Rob Cardwell
Jan Carey
Jennifer Carey
Daniel Carter
Michael Carter
Connor M Cartlidge
Chris Carver
Roberto Casado
Shea Castley Swain
Jake Cater-Bassett
Joshua Catten
David Cattermole
Charles J. Chan
Jeffrey Chan
Michael Chan
Luke Channell
Aylwin Chee
Chan Fai Chee
Larry Chen
Stephen Cheng
Nathaniel Chesney
Simpson Cheung
Chayang Chinpinkliew
Kyu-Hyung Cho
Robin Choi
Matthew Hwor Shen Chong
Alexander Choy
Paul Chrimes
Nicole Hendo Chu
Brett Chua
Pirayu Chuenkul
Michael Christopher Clark
Neil Clark
Aiden Clarke
Aria Rae Clarke
Elliott-James Clarke
Nigel Coady
Keith Coker
Allan Cole
Matt Colley
Niall Collings
Liz Collingwood
Alex Collins
Brian Gerald Collins
Paul and Brian Collins
Alan Colquhoun
Jingtan Cong
Joe Connolly
Joseph Connolly
Colin Connor
John Constant
Mark Constant
Calum Cook
John Coombs
Liam Cooper
Paul Cooper
Adam Cordery
Sandra Cornelius
Allan Corrigan
Henry Costo
James Cotter
Stan Cottrell
Albert Stanley Cragg
Henry Crawford
Lawrence and Rosina Cross
Luke Croucher
John Culshaw
Joe Curran
Tom Curran
Jan Currie
Joel Cussons
Vilas Dabasia
Richard Dance
Mark Daniels
Brendan Jodi Darcy Roche
Fred Dare
David Daulby
Chris Davies
Dan Davies
Frank Davies
Joe Davies
Logan Davies
Paul Davies
Ricki Davies
Rob Davies
Joseph De Benedictis
Andrew Deacon
Phil Deakin
Gerard Dee
Emma Deeks
Steven Deeks
Carlo Delas Alas
Danny Dempsey-Parr
Bryan Denny
Dalglish Dhanda
Kevin Dielenberg
Ralph Donald
Marc Douwen
John Dower
Stacey and David Dowling
Frank and Tony Doyle
Mick Doyle
Frank Draper
Natalie Drummond
Stephen Duffin
Iain Duffy
Robert Duffy
Sean Duffy
Kevin Eccles
Jim and Will Edgar
James Edwards
Laurence Edwards
Nick, Mandy and Rhys Edwards
Ian Eggleton
Henrik Eigenbrod
Steve Ellis
Holly Evans
Katie Evans
Lee John Evans
Darren Eyles
Sean Fadden
David Fairhurst
Mary Fairhurst
Nigel Fairhurst
Chua Family
Kusabs Family
John Farrell
Martyn Farrell
Eric Fearon
Michael Jan Ferreira
Joseph Ferry
Reuben Fifield
Anthony Filby
Rita Finlay
Eddie Fitzgerald
Declan Fogarty
Adam Paul Fogerty
B J Fong
Edwin Fong
John Paul Edmund Foo
Reds Foreman
Joseph Formosa
Alex Forrest
John Forrest
Mike Forrest
Lee Foster
Jonathan Fowler
Joe Foy
OLSC France
Freedom Frost
Mikaele Frost
Haslan Farouk Fuad
Sarah Fudge
Wuttichai Fufuangmongkolkit
Faith Fulcher
Anita Fung
Jevgenijs Galkins
Jack Gant
Oscar Garay
Carol Gardiner
Ian Gardiner
Liam Garvey
Sean Garvey
Jason Gates
Roy Gates
Allison Gavin
Mario Georgiades
Kenny Giles
Aaron Gilfoyle
Alison Gilfoyle
Bethany Gilfoyle
Carmen Gilfoyle
Carol Gilfoyle
Connor Gilfoyle
Holly Gilfoyle
Kevin Gilfoyle
Roy Gilfoyle
Samuel Gilfoyle
William Gilfoyle
Emma Gillan
Regan Gillies
Alan James Gilliland
Valerie Gilliland
Gunnar Ginebra
Simon Gonsalves
Luke Goodere
Amin Gopalani
David Gould
Aaron Gouthwaite
Cayden-Paul Gouthwaite
Geoffrey Gouthwaite
Lesley Gouthwaite
Paul Gouthwaite
Harold Gouthwaite Snr
Navinthran Govindasamy
Carol Graham
Jay Graham
Jennifer Graham
Fletcher Greenwood
David Greig
Jat Grewal
Jack James Castanheira Griffiths
Mathew Griffiths
Justin Grose
Keith Grundy
Luqman Guee
Brian Gunning
Christoph Haas
John Hagan
Mark E J Hamilton

THE FANS

Nazlin Hamzah
A Hyun Han
Henry Eileen Han
Seong Hyeok Han
Peter Hardacre
Richard Hardacre
Charlie Harding
Lee Hargreaves
David Harrison
Nicholas Harrison
Keith Hartley
Zainal Abideen Hassan
Thomas Hatley
Adrian Hawes
Kevin Hayden
Ruaridh Hayton
Angus Hayward
Charles Hayward
Eleanor Hayward
Georgina Hayward
Will Hearley
Matthew Heath
Sarah Heath
Hollie Hedley
Neil Hedley
Jeroen Heijink
Ola Helgedagsrud
Noah Hendry
Myra Hensley
Ian Hepworth
Ryan Herman
Bobby Hersey
Tom Heske
Darren Heslop
Harry Highton
Douglas Hill
Tony Hillman
John Hinchliffe
Michael Hinden
Frederic Hinnekens
Mark Hitchman
Lindsay Zaida Hitchon
Michael Hollan
Shane Holmes
Edward Hopkins
Gareth Hopkins
Jack Horsley
Wayne Horton
Trevor Hosford
Kwang Yeong How
Max Howard
Thomas Howden
Guang Hu

Adam Hughes
Michelle Hughes
Neil Hughes
Mike Humphreys
Elliot Hurst
Chas Hynes
Cormac Hynes
James Hynes
John Hynes
Kate Iddon
Koichi Ikejima
Angie Ineson
Kritpad Inphakdee
Gareth Irons
Tracey Isted
Bobster J
Michael Jackson
Peter Jackson
Dr Ampun Janpengpen
Ruth Jaques
Zayid Jathoonia
Thanya Jatuprayoon
Tanapat Jearanai
Daniel James Jenkins
Mark Andrew Jenkins
Todd Luca Jenkins
Sang Yoon Jeong
Yu-Bong Jeong
Bhatapong Jivavatanasak
Jirasuk Jivavatanasuk
Young-Doh Jo
George Johnson
Harry Johnson
Jeff Johnson
Mark Johnson
Steven Johnson
Andrew Johnston
Logan Joiner
Christopher Joint
Alan Jones
Ashley Jones
Finley Jones
Heath Jones
John Jones
Libby Jones
Megan Jones
Merewyn Jones
Michael Jones
Patricia Jones
Peter Jones
Stephanie Jones
Tessa Jones
Tony Jones

Tristan Jones
Yvonne Jones
Sam Judge
Colin Kangaloo
Anees Kathrada
Daniel Katz
Damian Kay
Dan Kay
Pauline Keating
Tony Kehoe
Callum Kelly
Tim Kelly
Jim Kemp
Janette Kemp
Alastair Kennedy
Robin Kennedy
Ava Kennerley
Harry Kennerley
Paul Kennerley
Sam Kennerley
Connor Kenyon
Jack Kerr
Claire Kerslake
William Kewn
Ryan Kilroe
Eunhye Kim
Gee Syub Kim
Chris King
Bradley Kingham
Alex Kirkham
Andrew Kiveal
Alexander Kiveal-Duffy
Chad Klythom
Tony Knox
Jan Ove Knudseth
Alexander Knyaginichev
Chadwyn Koh
John Koh
Lewis Krater
Phil Krater
Peter Kristine
Dave Kristy
Joe Kwan
Lim Kwan Hin
광균 Kwang-Kyun
Julian Kwong
Edwin Laboy
Abdilla Lahuddin
Andrew Laing
Dermot S Lally
Lam Yat Long
Lam Yat Hei
Brión Lawless

Jean Lazenby
Sebastian John William Le Sauvage
Gwanhyeong Lee
Elaine Leigh
Waratorn Lertwongweerachai
Dick Leung
Marcus Leung
Peter Leung
BK Lian
Alexander Liatis
Kahchi Liew
Mal Lightbourne
Miah Wee Lim
Richard Lim
Karl Lindsay
Peter Lindsey
Wills 28/11/05 Llewellyn
Wai Yip Lo
Darien Loh
Esther Lois
Lacretia Loke
William Loo
Brian Looker
Nathalie Lorent
Laura Lounds
June Love
David Lovenbury
Patrick Lucas
Tzeshan Lucas Victor Fung
Steven Lumley
Jonny Lund
Rasheed Lung
Darren Lyon
Joe Lyons
Murdoch Macdonald
Joe Magee
Colin Maguire
Andrew Major
Chris Mak
Michael Makison
Max Mallen-Freeman
Justin Mann
Manjit Singh Mann
Julien Marchand
Andy Marsden
Ben Marsden
Logan Marsh
Damian Martin
James Mason
Alby Mason
John Matheos
Graham Mathers
Terje Mathiassen

Luca Matta
Bill Matthews
Lee Mazurek
Aaron MC Namara
Linda McCann
Benjamin Luke McChrystal Plimmer
Daniel Edward McChrystal Plimmer
Hanna McChrystal Plimmer
James David McChrystal Plimmer
Vicky McClarron
Harry McConnachie
Alexander James McDonald
Andrew James McDonald
Robert Gordon McDonald
Shane McDonnell
Duncan McEwan
James McGee
Kieran McGeorge
William McGinnigle
Jack McGowan
Dean McGuinness
Gerry McGuinness
Joyce McGuinness
Samantha McGuinness
Shirley McGuinness
Brian McLean
Conor McLean
Lee McLinden
Andrew McLoughlin
James McLoughlin
Lucy McLoughlin
Prisca McLoughlin
Rebecca McLoughlin
Ava McNally
Harry McNally
Dean McNally
Liam McNeely
John McQueen
Harry Meijer
Thorsten Meiritz
Jamie Michaelson
James Middleton
Malcolm Middleton
Ross Middleton
Vanessa Middleton
Dan Miles
Katy Miles
Stuart Miles
Jared Miller
Pete Miller
Scott Mills
Kevin Milward
Chris Miranda

Georgie Mitchell
John Mitchell
Zariful Mohamed
Catherine Mok
Francis Monaghan
Issy Monaghan
John Monaghan
Max Monaghan
Ged Montgomery
Mark Montgomery
AJJK Moore
Patsy Moran
Andrew Morgan
Daniel Morgan
Ollie Morgan
Steve Morgan
Luke Moring
Andrew Morton
Jayne Morton
Jonathan Mountford
Daniel Mulhearn
Tim Mulrey
Edwin Munandar
Elizabeth Murphy
Greg Murphy
Jasmin Murphy
Joe Murphy
Oscar Murphy
Stephen Murphy
Tazio Muschi
Tony Musker
Jaewoo Nam
Ellya Abdullah Nambiar
Eddie Navarro
Tim Nelson
George Nestorovski
Daniel Ng
Kin Pong Ng
James Nicholson
Michael Nickson
Sharon Niehaus
Andreas Nilsson
Brian Nocera
David Nolan
Kenny Nolan
Millie Nolan
Joe Nuttorn
Snorre Andreas Nyeggen
Michael O'Connor
Ste O'Reilly
Kyran O'Brien
Michael Olsan
Suleyman Umit Onan
Phil Osborn
Rhys Osborne
Daniel Owen
Rhys Llewelyn Owen
John Owens
Michael Owery
Andrew Padley
Caroline Paget
Pali Palamathanan
Tak Pang
Solomon Papaloizou
Malcolm Parfett
Ben Park
Sunghyun Park
Barry Parker
Mary Ann Parker
Anna Parkinson
Alexander Parr
Thomas Parr
James Parry
Zenadin Patel
Ross Patterson
Tristan Paul Caple
Allister Payne
Matthew Peace
Jesper Pedersen
Ilan Peerutin
David Penhaligon
Paul Penketh
Brian Peters
Brian Phillips
Darren J Phillips
Gary Phillips
Surachest Phornsuwannapha
Jimmy Pilnick
Ernie Pinch
Adrian Pinfield
Samir Pirwany
Andrew Pitman
Mark Platt
Joel Terence John Plimmer
Jir6dech Pon6pun
Yuttachai Ponlakhan
Lisa Pope
Jamie Potts
Sam Alexander Powell
Frank Prade
A. Devin Pranata
Rangga Pratama
Daniel Preece
Lee Prescot
Steve Prescott
Denis Price
Junior Joseph Price
Katie Price
Maurice Price
Phil Price
Gary Prior
Paul Pritchard
Yuri Pronkin
Iwan Pugh
Thomas Wyn Pugh
Apirat Pun6ueb
Stephen Purcell
Tim Quadling
Seán Rafferty
Rahul Rahul
Ben Ralf
Hendrix Ramsey
Charlie Randles
David Randles
Joshua Randles
Apichai Raomanachai
Bob Reason
Alex Reid
Mary Reidy
Luke Reilly
Keith Rennie
Roger Rex
Kenneth Reynolds
William Rice
Darren Richardson
Dave Richardson
Dominic Richardson
Ian Richardson
Jack Richardson
Jason Ridley
Mark, Jo and Alex Ridout
Piyawat Riendechawetchakul
Patricia Riley
Frank Rimmer
Phil Rimmer
Jørgen Ringestad
Amy Roberts
David A Roberts
Eleanor Roberts
Jason Roberts
Steven Roberts
David Francis Roberts
Ken Robertson
Luke Robertson
Luke Snr Robertson
James Roche
Peter Roche
Robert Rodmell
Matthew Roe
John Rollo Rollinson
Patrick Rookes
Phil Rooney
Danielle Rose Watson
Austin Rothwell
Joel Round
Peter Rowan
Imogen Ryan
Jihoo Ryoo
Kanghyun Ryu
Misba Saheed
Steve Sahonta
Bobby Samra
Mark Sanders
Parin (First) Sanoonrat
Pratya Saringkharn
Kieron Savage
Christian Schmitz
Ian Scholes
James Schorah
James Scott
Alex Scouler
Adam Scrutton
Bailey Secker
Kevin Seddon
Andy Senyszyn
Hasan Shafi
Daanish Shahid
Adam Sharp
Philip Shaw
Phil Sheehan
Jeoffrey Sheen
Richard Shepherd
Robert Sheridan
Simon Shiels
Jackie Shin
Alan Shropshire
Bob Shrubb
Raspal Singh Sidhu
Roger Silson
King Huei Sim
Sunghoon Sim
Alan Simpson
Andy Simpson
Joshua Simpson
Harpreet Singh
Rajpal Singh
Marut Sirirat-At-Sadon
Jake Sisler
Luke Sisler
Paul Sisler
George Skandalellis
Samuel Skinner
John Slater
Ben Smedley
Barry Smith
Dean Smith
Gemma Smith
Lee Smith
Liam Smith
Madison Smith
Mark Smith
Peter Jason Smith
Stanley Robin Smith
Stephen Smith
Eoin Soulsbury
John Sowerby
Alex Spencer
Chris Daniel Robbie Spragg
Theo Squires
Rocco Staerk
Harrison Staines
Claire Standish
Myles Standish
Sadie Standish
Maciek Starczewski
Dan Stead
Philip Stearn
Diane Steel
Iain Steel
Kevin Stenhouse
Zackary Stephenson
Colin Stewart
Douglas Stirling
Euan Stirling
Ivo Stirling
Stuart Stirling
Clare Stocker
Dr Dirk Stromberg
Kevin Styles
Jayaraja Subramaniyan
Christopher Sullivan
Phil Summerfield
Craig Sumner
Alana Sumpter
Ben Sumpter
Colin Sumpter
Debra-Lea Sumpter
Ian Sumpter
Ian George Sumpter
Jake Sumpter
John Sumpter
Kathleen Sumpter
Kevin Sumpter
Natthaphol Suntudkarn
Alasdair Sutton

THE FANS

Ernie Sutton
Michael Sutton
Simon Sutton
Francis Sutton
Chee Kean Tan
Robert Tarrington
Scott Taylor
James 'Jimmy' Taylor
Shirley Luck Taylor
Pichayanin (Mild) Teerakraveekul
Rapeeporn Temeesak
Nicholas Tgb (SML BUNNIES)
Thossapol Themna
Stéphane Thévenet
Andrew Thomas
Craig Thomas
David Thomas
Helen Thompson
Joseph Thompson
Lewis Greer Thompson
Emma Tierney
Owen Timson
Marco Tonchi
Billy Tonge
John - Paul Tooley
Eric Torrey
Hadrien Touraud
Chris Towle
Mark Trevena
Yu Ming Tsang
George Tsartas
Chris Tynan
Alim Uddin
Karan Uka
Christopher Uren
John Uren
Joe and Andrew Valenti
Pat Veach
Scott Veach
Larry Vella
George Venios
Nick Verrall
Pawish Virajsilp
Tor Henrik von der Ohe
Sri Wahyudi
Brian Wainwright
Andy Wake
Andrew Walker
Robert Walsh
Dirk Walter
Marc Walter
Desmond Wan Wee Min
Jon Day Wanda
Supakij Wangdumrongves
Anuchit Wangthong
Craig Warcup
Paisley Ware
Andy Waring
Craig Warman
Thomas Francis Waters
Tommy Tate Waters
Robert Watkinson
Chloe Watson
Philip Watson
Scott Watson
Laurence Weaver
Stephen Webster
Steve Weidner
Marie Wells
Bradley Jaxon Welsh
Chris Welsh
Connor Welsh
Jamie Welsh
Rob Welsh
Ellen Westhead
Ann White
Chris Whitehead
David Whitehouse
Clive Whiteside
John Wibberley
Ryan Wiebe
Philip Wignall
Tim Wilding
Paul Wildridge
Jack Wilkinson
Harvey Willacy
Daz Williams
John G Williams
Kev Williams
Les Williams
Paul Williams
Tracy and Neil Williams
Archie Wilson
Dominic Wilson
Matt Wilson
Susan Wilson
Andrew Winder
Markus Windler
Porntep Wisarnthammakorn
Juliette Witek
Udomrit Witoonchawalitwong
Yoav Wolanski
Jinhee Won
Szelong Wong
Megan Wood
Shawn Wood
Andrew Wooding
Senan Woods
Stephen Woods
Andrew Woolley
Charlton Xerri
Peter Xiouri
Zixian Yang
Guo Lin Yao
Zm Yeap
Seung Joon Yeo
Yien Hoe Yeo
Lim Yew Mun
Sungwon Yoon
Kiril Yordanov
Shirley Young
Bertha Yu
Mustajab Zaidi
Mark Zajac
Henry Zeffman
Junjie Zhang
David Zhou
Antoni Zmaczynski
Γεωργιος Χρυσοστομακης